This book is the property of

_____

RELATIONSHIPS

THE VISUAL BOOK
FOR TEENS AND TWEENS

Boulder, CO

Contents

Chapter 1. The Foundation of Relationships

Chapter 2. Me and Myself

Chapter 3. Me and My Family

Chapter 4. Me and My Friends

Chapter 5. Me and My Romantic Partners

Chapter 6. Me and My Crew

Chapter 7. Me and the World

Why Should I Read This Book?

"Why don't they want to talk to me? Is something wrong with me?"

"Everyone says, 'Love yourself, and the world will love you back.' But how do I do that?"

"My parents don't understand me. How should I communicate with them?"

"I'm in love… Should I open up?"

We're all caught up in a complex network of relationships: with our family, friends, loved ones, our social circle. And, of course, with ourselves. Sometimes, it feels like we can't navigate this web — communication is challenging, mutual understanding seems elusive, and the fear of making mistakes and the pain of loneliness are always present.

But relationships are one of life's biggest sources of joy. They empower us, boost our self-confidence, and inspire us to achieve. Only through meaningful connections can we accomplish something powerful and truly understand ourselves.

This book will provide answers to your questions about relationships. Each page offers practical advice about how to love yourself, form friendships, connect with someone special, communicate with your parents, fit in with a group, and live in harmony with yourself and the world around you.

While this book doesn't contain much text, it's brimming with substance.

It delves into essential topics in an engaging and thought-provoking manner. Plus, it features numerous illustrations to help you connect to the content. You can read it from start to finish or jump to the section that interests you most.

So, are you ready to dive into the world of relationships?

CHAPTER 1
The Foundation of Relationships

- Why Relationships Matter

- How to Build Healthy Relationships

- When Relationships Feel Stressful

- Communication — the Foundation of Relationships

- Understanding Others

- Dealing with Conflicts

- Five Ways to Resolve Conflict

- *What's Next?*

Why Relationships Matter

Relationships… the happiness that comes from spending an entire day with your friends. The feeling of being supported after a heart-to-heart with your mom. The deep pain of breaking up with someone you love. Relationships are the most crucial and significant part of our lives. They're the threads that intertwine all aspects of our lives: work, school, personal life, and hobbies. Yet, we often chalk it up to luck when we have a good family or true friends. So, what role should we play in building strong connections?

The Secret to a Happy Life

Harvard scientists spent a remarkable 85 years studying the life paths of 724 people, all in pursuit of revealing the secrets of happiness, well-being, and health. What they discovered was groundbreaking but something we have all inherently known since childhood — the happiest moments stem from connecting with our parents or playing with our siblings and friends.

The key component in the recipe for human happiness is deep, warm relationships! Loneliness and social isolation don't just affect your personality; they harm your health. No amount of material wealth can ever provide the same enduring satisfaction that good relationships can.

So, if you find yourself focusing overly hard on chasing those big dreams, keep in mind the following:

People in happy relationships live a whole decade longer than those who remain alone.

Those who find their place within their local community or family experience fewer illnesses and enjoy a longer life.

When older individuals reflect on their most cherished life achievements, relationships with spouses, friends, family, and coworkers are consistently at the top of the list.

In the grand scheme, giving in relationships is just as vital as receiving. Many people see helping others as the pinnacle of their lives.

Does this mean you should abandon your ambitions, career goals, and education, and obsess over relationships as if they're the only worthwhile pursuit? Absolutely not. But there are two crucial takeaways here:

Don't neglect your relationships in favor of other life tasks, no matter how important or urgent they may seem. This choice won't bring you any extra happiness (or better health).

Relationships deserve your attention just as much as your job, education, and personal goals do. Dedicate time to your relationships. Building them requires a mindful effort.

You're the Architect of Your Relationships

Think of relationships as bridges constructed by people reaching out to each other. It's crucial to build and maintain them from both ends. Your relationship bridges can come in all shapes and sizes.

Some may be unstable or even hazardous — you'll become skilled at identifying and dismantling those in time.

Others may crumble unexpectedly or erode gradually under life's pressures — but you'll have the inner strength and self-belief to weather those separations and losses.

Some will form out of a simple, fleeting encounter or conversation and lead you to individuals who can change your life.

And then there will be those that can withstand any storm and become your rocks — learn to treasure and fortify such relationships.

First, you have to lay the foundation within yourself: learn to accept and love who you are. Then, you extend that foundation to your inner circle — your family, friends, and significant other. After that, you expand these skills to encompass the entire world, forging relationships with society. It all boils down to you, as you build each relationship brick by brick with your own two hands.

How to Build Healthy Relationships

Some relationships are like strong winds pushing you forward, albeit with a few bumps along the way, while others are like anchors that hold you back or weigh you down. What defines good and not-so-good connections?

Recognizing Healthy and Not-So-Healthy Relationships

Every relationship is unique based on the people involved, and it can have a big impact on you, either in a good or a not-so-good way.

Not-So-Healthy

Force you to pretend to be someone you're not.

Make you feel a heavy burden that you have to carry around and can't shed.

Drain your energy, leaving you tired and unmotivated.

Leave you alone to deal with problems.

Hold you back from growing, keeping you stagnant, or making you change in ways you don't like, **often with criticism or pressure.**

Healthy

Let you be you; you don't have to change or give up what's important to you.

Make you happy; you appreciate them, even if you have to end them someday.

Give you energy and inspire you to do positive things.

Make you feel supported when things get tough.

Help you grow, making you want to be a better version of yourself and move forward in life.

Sometimes, we settle for questionable relationships just to avoid feeling alone. But is it worth giving up the freedom to be yourself?

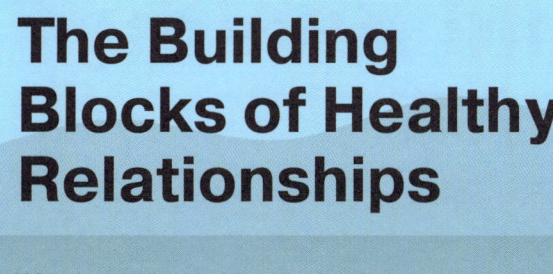

The Building Blocks of Healthy Relationships

Whether it's with friends, family, or someone special, all healthy relationships share the same basic principles. Here's what to look for:

Equality and Respect

It's all about treating each other with respect and knowing that everyone is equally important.

Understanding and Acceptance

You accept each other just the way you are; there's no need for either of you to change.

Honesty and Trust

No secrets, no lies. You trust each other and know you can count on one another.

Being Open and Authentic

You're real and open with each other, without any masks or pretending. Deep connections come from being yourself.

Safety and Personal Boundaries

You respect each other's personal space and don't push boundaries without asking first. You have friendly talks about what works and what doesn't without feeling guilty.

Being Kind and Caring Toward Each Other

You're there for each other, no matter what. You always consider each other's feelings and needs.

Selflessness and Willingness to Give

You put effort into the friendship without wanting something in return. It's all about giving, not keeping score.

So, which of these principles are essential parts of your relationships with your friends or significant others?

When Relationships Feel Stressful

Sometimes, relationships can feel like a slow poison, gradually affecting your well-being and distancing you from your true self. Let's explore what to do when your relationships with a partner, friends, or family aren't bringing you joy.

Identifying Unhealthy Relationships

If being in a relationship makes you feel worse than being alone, chances are it's an unhealthy one.

Within Unhealthy Relationships:

- Your mood takes a sharp downturn, and you feel drained.
- You are constantly walking on eggshells, fearing that you might say or do something wrong to upset your companion.
- Your needs and desires take a back seat.

- You're continually blamed for things.
- Your personal boundaries are disregarded.
- You sense an imbalance and lack of fairness.

Have you ever come across people in your life who made you feel something similar?

Three Red Flags of Manipulation

Unhealthy relationships often involve manipulation, and recognizing it isn't always easy. Sometimes, even the ones doing the manipulating don't realize they're trying to control others. However, understanding some common patterns can help you recognize and fight manipulation.

YOU SENSE THAT SOMETHING'S WRONG BUT CHOOSE TO IGNORE IT

Imagine you have a friend who is loudly criticizing someone's appearance, and you politely ask them to stop. In response, they get angry and accuse you of always complaining. Your day is ruined, but you'd rather not dwell on it. Sound familiar?

YOU CONSTANTLY FEEL GUILTY

Your grandma is upset because you can't help her fix her cabinet on your only day off. She scolds you, saying, "The neighbor's grandson visits her every day!" Tomorrow, you have an exam, so you can't go to a party. Your partner says, "You don't know how to have fun." You feel guilty, even though you're acting in your own best interests.

YOU FORGET WHO YOU ARE

When you go to the movies, it's always a film your friend wants to see. What do you enjoy? You can't even remember. Dad never asks what you want for dinner. It's always what he prefers. You've lost track of your own preferences and desires.

"Something's not right" doesn't always mean the relationships are unhealthy.
Before taking drastic steps, ask yourself:

1 **What exactly makes these relationships unhealthy?** If you simply feel they aren't ideal, it doesn't necessarily mean they're toxic.

2 **How valuable and significant are these relationships to you?** This determines whether you want to put in effort to improve them.

3 **Which aspects of these relationships depend on you, and which ones don't?** Try applying the principles of healthy relationships in your approach first.

4 **Has anything changed in the relationships over time?** If you've done everything in your power to make them healthier, yet they remain toxic, consider ending them.

What to Do with Unhealthy Relationships

If a relationship is tearing you apart, it's time to end it! But do so honestly and make it clear it's your choice, not their fault.
While ending a relationship, don't carry the heavy burden of disappointment and resentment with you. If you do, this relationship will continue to poison your life.

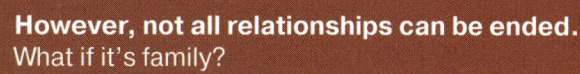

However, not all relationships can be ended.
What if it's family?

Speak up about your feelings and what's happening. For instance, if your mom claims you never help with cleaning or cooking, explain that it's hurtful to hear such things. Give her examples of past times when you did help and explain why you can't assist her right now.

Firmly decline to act if someone suggests something that goes against your interests, values, or beliefs.

Accept that some people don't want to change. Everyone has different experiences; perhaps they don't know how to handle their emotions. It doesn't mean they wish you harm; often, they think they're acting out of love.

Reduce the time spent with people who refuse to change their behavior even after you kindly ask them to do so.

Communication — the Foundation of Relationships

Staying close to people means communicating with them. So, don't be surprised if a friend you haven't called or texted in ages sounds distant. How you talk to each other can make or break your relationships. So, how do we communicate?

Your Inner Circle

It might seem like we're constantly surrounded by communication, but most of it, around 90%, is just surface-level stuff that comes up during work or school. Research has shown that, on average, people maintain deep and meaningful conversations with only 10-15 people from their inner circle. That's why talking to those close to us is so important. After all, the quality of our conversations plays a big role in our overall happiness.

Who is in your inner circle?

Types of Communication

Communication isn't just about words spoken aloud or typed in a chat. We connect on different levels, offering emotional support and sharing energy. It's this well-rounded kind of communication that brings real satisfaction.

Words, Words, Words…

Any message we deliver with words has two parts: what we say (the content) and how we say it (the way it's presented). For healthy communication, it's just as important to consider HOW you say something as WHAT you're saying.

WHAT (Content): Asking your younger brother to clean up after himself.

HOW 1 (Form 1): "Could you please clean up after yourself?"

HOW 2 (Form 2): "You've made a mess again. How many times do I have to ask you to clean up?"

Which way would help your brother understand your request better?

6 Guidelines for Healthy Communication

When you talk to someone, remember to:

- Be open, genuine, and honest. Trust starts here.

- Show kindness and care. It's the foundation of love.

- Demonstrate interest and understanding. It's a sign of respect.

- Help each other grow and give constructive feedback. That's showing you care.

- Express gratitude. It makes people feel valued.

- Stay in touch frequently and consistently. That's what keeps things steady.

Remember, the depth of communication is more important than its duration. If you've got 10 minutes, it's better to use them for a deep conversation about something that truly matters.

Often, we're afraid our words will hurt the other person, but more often than not, it's the way we say them that stings.

Gestures, Facial Expressions, Tone

Psychologist Albert Mehrabian once said that when we're emotionally connecting in person, 55% of the message's meaning comes from nonverbal cues (like gestures, facial expressions, tone of voice, eye contact, etc.), 38% from our voice and how we say things, and only 7% from the actual words.

Facial Expressions: The emotions on our faces, including changes in facial muscles and eye movements.

Gestures: Hand and body movements, including finger motions.

Tone of Voice: The way we speak, including intonation, pitch, speed, volume, and pauses.

Body Poses and Movements: How we position ourselves and our movements, such as leaning or gesturing.

Eye Contact: Where we look and how long we hold someone's gaze.

Personal Space: The distance between people and how they're positioned relative to each other.

In open, relaxed conversations, we use broad gestures, our posture is relaxed, we smile, and make direct eye contact. However, factors like age or personality can sometimes get in the way. For example, if we're feeling shy, we might avoid eye contact and keep our distance. Others might interpret these signals as unfriendly, even if our words say otherwise. What's the solution? Consciously adjust our nonverbal cues.

Emotions

We can pick up on someone's emotions just by being around them, without even saying a word. A room with a tired dad feels heavy like the air is thick with exhaustion. On the other hand, at your best friend's place, you get nothing but positive vibes.

The emotions we share with others depend on our **emotional hygiene.** That's right, managing your emotions is like washing your hands regularly!

- **Pay attention to your emotions:** what makes you feel a certain way and why? Don't bottle up or ignore unpleasant emotions. They'll build up and create tension or lead to a blow-up and conflict.
- **Express your emotions honestly and directly,** but do it with kindness and consideration.
- **Steer clear of criticizing** or judging others.
- **Respect other people's boundaries.**
- **And don't forget about self-respect.** You have the right to your emotions and opinions, and no one should deny them or pressure you to change.

Actions Speak Louder Than Words

Showing you care by doing things like making tea, washing the dishes, or cooking dinner is also a form of communication. Doing things together — like going hiking or working on a project — can bring people closer than a bunch of words.

The more ways you communicate in a relationship, the stronger and closer it becomes. Don't try to save time on meaningful communication in all its forms with people from your close circle because this interaction is the foundation of your relationships.

Understanding Others

Communication plays a massive role in our lives. But often, it seems more like a bunch of voices, each one talking about different stuff. As a result, people end up wasting time without really understanding each other or offering support. So, how can we make our conversations deeper and more productive?

Communication: A Basic Human Need

Understanding what others are thinking and feeling, and having them know us is something everyone needs. We don't simply chat for no reason; genuine conversations are essential for building authentic connections.

To get better at deep conversations, you need to develop two key skills, like you would tend to two plants in your garden: active listening and empathy. If you take good care of them and keep nurturing them, you'll find it easier to connect with people.

Active Listening: I Hear You

A lot of times, we listen to someone, but we don't really hear them. We get lost in their emotions and don't pay attention to what they're saying. Sometimes, we're too wrapped up in our own thoughts and reactions, and we miss the true meaning of what the other person is trying to say. Active listening, where you give your full attention and genuine interest to the speaker, can help you tune in to their wavelength. Here's how you can develop this skill:

Stay focused and clear your mind. Look into the speaker's eyes, not around the room or at your phone. Try not to let your thoughts wander away from the conversation. You can even silently repeat the last word the speaker said.

Listen without making judgments. Try not to label or jump to conclusions as you listen. Don't let those weeds flourish in the conversation garden. Just listen and remember.

Don't interrupt. It might seem like interrupting shows you're interested and paying attention, but it usually comes across as disrespectful.

Ask questions to get more details. Different people attach different meanings to the same words. At first, you might not get the true meaning of a word, and then there might be another one, and soon you can't share the speaker's experience, and vice versa.

Do you find this problematic? If so, why? Which of these techniques already works well for you?

Empathy: Stepping into Their Shoes

The second flower in the garden of deep communication is learning to put yourself in someone else's shoes and understanding their feelings, interests, and needs.

1 What is the person feeling? Try to figure out the emotion your conversation partner is going through and why. Pay attention not only to their words, but also to their body language, like gestures, facial expressions, and posture. You can ask directly, "How are you feeling? What's got you thinking like this?"

2 Don't downplay their problems. If your friend talks about feeling tired, don't say, "Come on, it's not a big deal!" Instead, use phrases that show support, like, "Feeling tired is tough; I get why you'd feel that way."

3 Put yourself in their situation. Think about how you'd feel if you were dealing with the same thing.

4 Avoid criticism, even in your thoughts. Everyone has the right to their feelings and actions, both you and your conversation partners. Instead of getting annoyed or quickly making judgments, think about what might be causing their actions.

5 Show compassion, but don't suffer with them. Other people's choices aren't your burden, so don't take responsibility for them. Empathy is about understanding and supporting, not suffering.

Weeds in the Garden

To grow active listening and empathy, you need to spot and remove the weeds — negative attitudes that can pop up during conversations. Acknowledge them but don't let them take hold.

"I already know everything." During a conversation, you act like you already know what the other person will say. This makes it hard to understand the real meaning of their words.

"I'll respond later." Instead of listening, you mentally rehearse your replies.

"I'll give some advice now!" You try to offer advice and judgment when it's not asked for. Most of the time, people want to be heard and supported, not given advice and directions.

"Let me tell you my story!" You constantly want to insert your own story, not letting your conversation partner finish.

"I don't want to hear this." You reject what you don't like or don't want to hear.

How many weeds do you have in your communication garden?

Dealing with Conflicts

Not many people enjoy conflicts. They can be draining, nerve-wracking, and sometimes lead to a breakup. But, conflicts have a positive side if you approach them correctly. They can help build stronger relationships, assert your interests, and even help you understand each other better.

Why Conflicts Are Necessary

The root cause of arguments and conflicts is a clash of interests. When your friend wants to go to the movies, and you want to as well, you both simply buy your tickets. But when one of you wants to see a movie and the other wants to play games at home, that's a conflict of interests. The good news is that conflicts can be highly beneficial. They teach you how to negotiate, understand your interests better, and ultimately help relationships grow.

Arguing Just for the Sake of It

Often, we argue as if our lives depend on it, even when it's just a debate about a favorite YouTuber or where to go for a walk. We fight, get upset, and sometimes even end friendships over trivial matters. But most of the time, the essence of the conflict or winning the argument aren't worth losing a relationship or trust. In real life, we rarely find ourselves in an "all or nothing" situation where one person wins everything, and the other is left with nothing. The next time you find yourself in an argument with someone, ask yourself: is what we're arguing about really that important?

Fight, Flight… or Halt

Our bodies react to conflicts as stress and automatically trigger one of two responses.
Fight → You attack the other person, let your emotions take over, show aggression, or even physically fight with them.
Flight → You avoid the conflict: you change the subject, stay silent, or simply agree with everything the other person says.

But there's an alternative, non-automatic response.
Halt
The most productive reaction in a conflict is to understand that your body is reacting to stress and to take a break. This gives you time to reflect on what's happening, think, and choose a successful behavior strategy. The "halt" reaction can lead to constructive dialogue. When this happens, conflicts contribute to relationship growth rather than deterioration.

How to Avoid Automatic "Fight" or "Flight" Reactions

TAKE THREE DEEP BREATHS
Press pause on your stream of reactions, emotions, and chaotic thoughts.

ASK YOURSELF THE FOLLOWING QUESTIONS
- What feelings is this conflict triggering in me: anger, sadness, despair, fear?
- What interests are currently colliding?
- What do I want to achieve as a result of this argument? Maintain good relations, assert my interests (are they really all essential?), not waste time, etc.

START A DIALOGUE
Focus on the outcome you want. Ask the other person what they want. Try to create a safe atmosphere for both yourself and your conversation partner: don't yell, don't insult them, and stop if they insult you.

Initially, these three steps may require extra concentration and time. That's okay! Just tell your conversation partner that you need a couple of minutes to think. The more you use this method during arguments, the faster you'll make it through all the stages.

How do you usually react to an argument?

What to Say and How to Say It

It's easy to get stuck in a conflict and escalate the argument if you use specific techniques, phrases, and intonations. Try to avoid these triggers:

1 THE SUPERIOR POSITION (I'M BETTER, SO IT SHOULD BE MY WAY)
Ordering, threatening, mocking, or pointing out the other person's flaws shows disrespect, intensifies the dispute, and steers it away from constructive dialogue.

2 DECEPTION
Avoid lying or distorting information. You'll likely get caught in a lie, and future interactions won't go well. Besides, distorted information won't lead to conflict resolution.

3 IRRITATING WORDS
Try not to use words like "why," "always," "never," and "how many times." For example, saying "Why are you always late?" or "You never understand me!" oversimplifies the situation and doesn't address the root of the conflict. Instead, use the formula "I feel… because…" For example, "I feel hurt that you were late because I believe it shows a lack of respect."

4 MANIPULATION
It's easy to get what you want if you hold someone hostage. Phrases like "Our friendship will be over" or "I won't go to the party with you then" are manipulative and, when overused, can destroy any relationship.

Five Ways to Resolve Conflict

We all go through our fair share of conflicts, ranging from minor disagreements to significant clashes that can drag on. It's essential not to get anxious about them, but to learn how to navigate these situations with acceptable outcomes.

Psychologists Kenneth Thomas and Ralph Kilmann came up with five strategies for handling conflicts. Each one can be valuable, depending on what you aim to achieve. It's crucial to consider the appropriate strategy only after you've managed to avoid the automatic "fight" or "flight" responses.

Competition

WHEN AND HOW TO USE IT

You can't compromise on your interests because the conflict involves something critical and fundamental. You need to assert your point of view using all available means, from outright refusal to considering other proposals. One good example of this is a debate club or a math competition, where this strategy is fully utilized. It's essential to remember that competition doesn't imply rudeness or unfriendliness.

PROS

You can fully defend your interests.

CONS

Relationships can sour and even end. Before choosing competition, think carefully about whether your position is genuinely fundamental and unwavering.

Avoidance

WHEN AND HOW TO USE IT

You don't see any real importance in the issue causing disagreement, so you don't have the time, desire, or energy to address it, and you choose to ignore it. For example, someone accidentally bumped into you in line, but you'd rather not get into a confrontation, so you decide to let it slide.

PROS

Sometimes, like in the example, avoiding a conflict is more productive than engaging in it. This way, you save time, energy, and unnecessary stress. Occasionally, conflicts can resolve themselves if you just wait it out.

CONS

Not all conflicts fade away on their own. If you keep ignoring your mom's requests to tidy up your room, it could lead to a big argument. So, opt for avoidance only when the conflict definitely won't have consequences.

Accommodation

WHEN AND HOW TO USE IT

You currently value mutual understanding more than the subject of the conflict. You want to avoid further confrontation and decide it's better to yield or try to evade trouble. For instance, if a school administrator asks you a few questions about your absence: there's no point in arguing here.

Compromise

WHEN AND HOW TO USE IT

Both sides of the conflict arrive at a solution that partially satisfies each party. For example, you want to go to a horror movie, and your friend wants to see a romantic comedy. In the end, you decide on an action-adventure film.

PROS

You maintain good relationships, avoid unnecessary stress, and partially fulfill your expectations or get something particularly valuable by giving up something secondary.

CONS

Compromise often leads to an uneven solution, and you might feel like your interests have taken a back seat.

Collaboration

WHEN AND HOW TO USE IT

This strategy is also known as a "win-win." The issue is so vital to the conflict's participants that a suitable solution must be found for everyone involved. It's the most labor-intensive, yet productive strategy: it requires time for constructive discussion and being honest and open about expectations. However, everyone ends up benefiting from it.

PROS

The interests of all parties are fully taken into account. Your relationships enter a new level of understanding. Collaboration is often the only correct strategy in deep relationships where the conflict touches on important matters for both partners. Only through constructive dialogue and accepting each other's ideas can a group emerge from a crisis and strengthen their relationship.

CONS

This strategy requires your time and effort. Ask yourself: is the point of the conflict worth such efforts?

PROS

You maintain good relationships and do something nice for the other person. You don't waste your energy on competition. You avoid trouble.

CONS

The more you agree, the greater the chances your interests will continue to be disregarded. Your self-esteem may decrease, and people may stop listening to your opinion. Choose "accommodation" only when your principles and key interests won't be harmed.

What's next?

Take a moment to think:

- Do you have healthy relationships in your life? What about unhealthy ones?

- Think about the people you feel most comfortable with. What makes these relationships so comfortable?

- Do you often clutter the meaning of your words or make generalizations?

- How did you react in a recent conflict: fight, flight, or stay calm?

Reading material:

- "Nonviolent Communication: A Language of Life: Life-Changing Tools for Healthy Relationships" by Marshall B. Rosenberg

- "Getting to Yes: Negotiating Agreement Without Giving In" by Roger Fisher and William Ury

- "Games People Play: The Psychology of Human Relationships" by Eric Berne

- "Stillness Is the Key" by Ryan Holiday

Watch and learn:

Celeste Headlee's TED Talk on **"10 Ways to Have a Better Conversation"**

Julian Treasure's TED Talk on **"How to Speak So That People Want to Listen"**

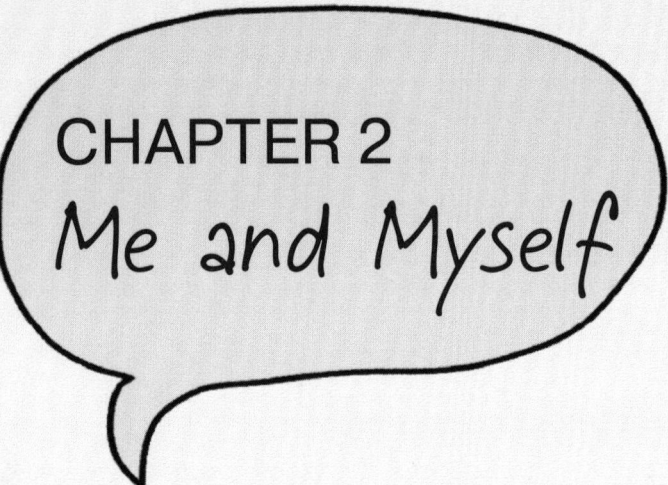

CHAPTER 2
Me and Myself

- It's All about Me

- The Role and Value of Ego

- My Self-Esteem

- Unconditional Self-Love

- Should I Fear Loneliness?

- Being Authentic

- *What's Next?*

It's All About Me

Alright, so let's talk about something super-important: me. Everything I've got starts with me. The only thing I can truly control is myself. I'm responsible for my actions and no one else's. Life is full of changes — moving, switching schools or jobs, breakups, and losses. But through it all, one person stays constant in my life, and that's me. That's why the relationship I have with myself matters the most. My whole life depends on the quality of that relationship.

WHY IS IT SO CRUCIAL TO START WITH A RELATIONSHIP WITH MYSELF?

Well, because I'm like the seed from which my entire world grows. I can relate to the world better when I understand and accept myself, with all my talents, quirks, and weaknesses. Plus, I won't be relying on other people's opinions of me or get thrown off course by temporary problems (at the very least, I'll have something to counterbalance that all with). Having a good relationship with myself is like having a home to come back to whenever I need to relax, recharge, or boost my confidence.

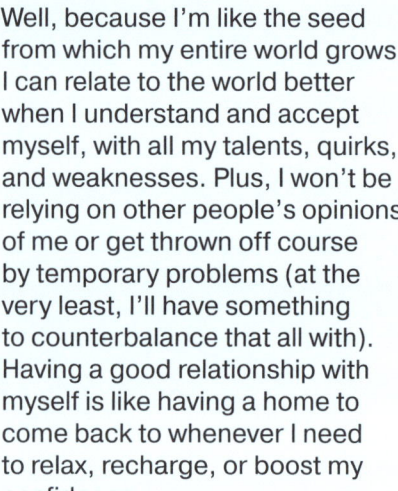

Is this true for you too?

Or do you feel like you're your own prison?

How did it come to this?

IT ALL STARTS WITH GETTING TO KNOW MYSELF. WHO AM I?

I spend most of the day in my own thoughts. Is that who I am? My own thoughts? But they're so fickle, and sometimes they get all mixed up with other people's thoughts. My head can be absolutely chaotic sometimes, with thoughts contradicting each other. However, I can stop or even change them!

People usually see my outward appearance first — my face, body, and how I move. Does this mean I am my own body? But I can change it, control it, and even if I lose or alter a part of it, I'm still me.

Maybe the feelings I have are what make me? But sometimes, I feel a whole bunch of emotions at once, and they disappear before I can even figure them out. At different times, I can feel both anger and love, hurt and gratitude. Who feels all of that?

It seems like I'm the one behind it all, the one who brings together my thoughts, emotions, and body into one, who can observe from the sidelines and change different parts of me, who can distinguish between good and bad, the one responsible for the harmony of all the pieces of my "me." People call this integral part the soul, some call it consciousness, and others might have different names for it. I'll just call it my inner "me" or... (insert any word that feels right to you).

I'M MORE THAN JUST MY THOUGHTS, EMOTIONS, AND BODY. BUT WHAT DOES THAT CHANGE?

If I were to observe myself long enough, I would see that my thoughts, emotions, and appearance are like ever-changing weather against the backdrop of my unchanging consciousness. This integral part of me, my inner "me," brings me peace and confidence. It doesn't judge me or others. It accepts me and the world as a whole. It's capable of love, forgiveness, and compassion, regardless of the ever-changing nature of my thoughts and emotions.

IF I LET THIS PART OF ME CREATE THE RULES OF MY LIFE — MY VALUES AND PRINCIPLES — IT MIGHT SOUND SOMETHING LIKE THIS:

- *I value life. I am life. Therefore, I value myself.*

- *I love people. I am a person. Therefore, I love myself.*

- *I believe that goodness is part of human nature. I am goodness.*

Values and principles are like my inner compass, helping me navigate through life. I use them to determine what's important and how to act in different situations, establish boundaries, and make decisions.

WHAT KIND OF RELATIONSHIP DO YOU WANT TO HAVE WITH YOURSELF?

I'm the only element in my life that I can fully control. That means I get to decide how I treat myself. If my relationship with myself were a home, I'd want it to be bright, warm, and cozy. I'd want it to be a place where I can always return, no matter the circumstances, a place that provides support and protection, a place where I want to live.

I'd also want to know and accept my principles, desires, and capabilities. I'd want to believe in my own "goodness" and remember that I can always rely on myself. I'd want to live in harmony with my values and not depend on others.

MY HARMONIOUS RELATIONSHIP WITH MYSELF, LIKE A PUZZLE, IS MADE UP OF PIECES THAT INCLUDE:

Imagine, just for a moment, that a group hungry for power is forcing their principles upon you.

How would those principles sound?

And how would they sound if you spend hours watching ads on social media?

What are YOUR values and principles?

Self-love

Self-acceptance and self-respect

Healthy self-esteem

The courage to be myself

So, what's holding you back from building this kind of relationship with yourself?

The Role and Value of Ego

Let's dive into something special: ego. Ever since I was a kid, I've heard that it's a bad thing, something we should hide away for the sake of loving others. Being selfish, doing things for our own interests, isn't usually seen as a good thing. But guess what? Ego exists for a reason, and it's not just me; everybody's got one. So, there's got to be more to it, right?

WHAT EXACTLY IS EGO, AND WHERE DOES IT COME FROM?

Ego is like the protective shell around my inner "me," keeping it safe from all the crazy stuff happening in the outside world. It's the mediator that allows my inner "me" to interact with the world without getting hurt or overwhelmed.

Ego starts forming around 6-9 months old, which experts like Jacques Lacan call the "mirror stage." That's when babies start recognizing themselves in a mirror and realizing they're separate from everyone else around them.

Once formed, ego helps me make choices and do things that match up with my goals and interests. It's what lets me set personal boundaries and say no to things I find unacceptable.

But ego can sometimes go from being a protector to a troublemaker if I forget its true job and mix it up with my inner "me." The nature of ego is to separate itself from others to keep me safe and independent. **Under the influence of ego, I might start thinking that the way I see the world is the same as reality.**

For example, I had a bad experience with dogs as a kid. My true "me" might actually be curious about and sympathetic toward dogs. But my ego, acting like a bodyguard, could keep warning me to stay away, making me believe that dogs are pure evil. If I let my ego completely take over, my caution could make me aggressive or hostile.

Have you ever met someone who reacts defensively at the slightest criticism? Is that their inner "me" or their ego? What is their ego trying to protect them from?

SO, HOW DO YOU BREAK FREE FROM THE CLUTCHES OF EGO? YOU GROW WITH IT!

Ego isn't like a costume you wear once and then throw away when you grow up. It's more like a process that keeps developing, according to psychologist Jane Loevinger. She came up with stages of ego development, which are like levels that help your inner "me" express itself fully, even by connecting with the world in a new way.

But is that true? Think back to times when your beliefs or lack of information made you see a situation differently from what was actually happening.

EGO DEVELOPMENT STAGES

1 INFANCY STAGE
The start of realizing you're a separate individual.

2 IMPULSIVE STAGE
Emotional reactions to things as either good or bad, right or wrong, or something to be praised or blamed for.

3 SELF-PROTECTIVE STAGE
Learning to control yourself, understanding rules and norms, and trying to get along with them.

4 CONFORMIST STAGE
Believing it's most important to belong to a group, seeing your and others' worth through group values and rules.

5 SELF-AWARE STAGE
Self-criticism and the ability to envision multiple possibilities in events are awakened. You are becoming more aware of the difference between the "real me" and the "expected me."

6 CONSCIENTIOUS STAGE
Starting to think about yourself and others more deeply, seeing reality from different angles. Most grown-ups over 25 are at this stage.

7 INDIVIDUALISTIC STAGE
Valuing individuality and breaking free from expectations and strict rules.

8 AUTONOMOUS STAGE
Thinking your self-realization is more important than how successful you look to others. You're willing to accept yourself just as you are. You deeply respect other people's independence, no matter how different they are.

9 INTEGRATED STAGE
Fully accepting yourself and others, showing compassion, and cooperation. This is the final stage of ego development, where you value your own and others' individuality, and you connect with the world not because you have to, but because you choose to.

NOW, LET'S TALK ABOUT EGOISM AND WHETHER IT SERVES ANY PURPOSE

We label behavior as egoistic when it ignores one person's interests in favor of another's. Egoism is doing things driven by your ego without considering what's going on with your inner "me."

For instance, imagine we're leaving a café together, and it starts raining. There's only one umbrella. I decide to keep it for myself because I don't want to catch a cold. My ego's not thinking about your health; it only cares about mine. If I don't get my ego in check, you might think that's just who I am.

But here's the twist: when I manage my ego the right way, it helps me meet my real needs.

For instance, a woman divorces her husband because he's disrespectful and rude. She feels torn about this egoistic decision (since it's all about her interests) because her child will have to adapt to a new life and rebuild her relationship with her dad. But a woman's decision is fueled by her inner need for respect and love.

So, which stage of ego development are you currently in? Do you know anyone who is at the autonomous or integrated stage? How do they express themselves?

So, next time you feel like calling someone selfish, remember that it's not always that simple. When you catch yourself being selfish, ask yourself who's in the driver's seat — your ego or your real inner needs.

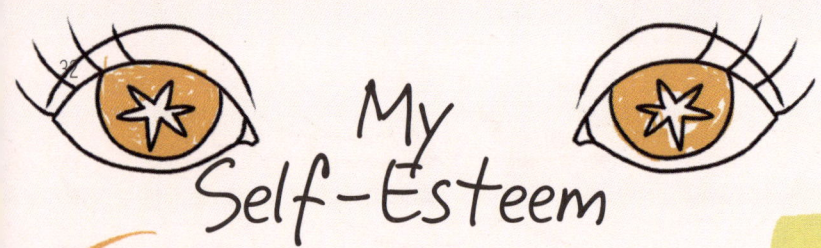

My Self-Esteem

How do I view myself when I'm all dressed up? What do others think of me when I make mistakes? I want to feel okay even when I don't look perfect or when I mess up. I want my self-esteem to be rock-solid and not dependent on social media likes, sideways glances, or criticism from others. So, how can I make that happen?

WHAT IS SELF-ESTEEM?

Self-esteem is how I feel about my own worth. It can either be steady, when I accept my value unconditionally, or it can vary depending on the situation and the people I'm with.

+

STEADY SELF-ESTEEM

This is the kind of self-esteem that allows me to feel confident no matter what's going on around me. It's the foundation of my self-worth. You can think of it like the average annual temperature on Earth — it's pretty consistent.

−

SITUATIONAL SELF-ESTEEM

This one might make me doubt myself or feel proud depending on the situation. It's like ever-changing weather, influenced by the seasons, weather patterns, and the time of day.

If I constantly focus on the "weather" of situational self-esteem and don't notice the "average temperature" of steady self-esteem, I'll always struggle with fluctuations in my self-worth.

Do you notice that your self-esteem changes?

When do you feel confident, and when do you doubt yourself?

HOW SELF-ESTEEM DEVELOPS

Steady self-esteem is built when I unconditionally accept my value and my right to exist. It's self-esteem born from my inner self. Every person is valuable and unique by nature, and I'm no exception. My principles, personal qualities, and interests create a unique combination — my unique personality. As an individual, I have just as much worth as anyone else on this planet.

Situational self-esteem is shaky, fragile, and dependent. I might view myself differently in various situations, but my inner essence — my unconditional self-worth — remains the same and can only grow with years, experience, and wisdom. So, why is it so hard for me to believe that?

SELF-ESTEEM AND THE OPINIONS OF OTHERS

It's easy to believe what others think about me. It often seems like their view is more objective. But external criticism is just the opinion of one person or a group. It's often a reflection of the critic's own life experience, beliefs, and mood.

People are going to criticize me, and I can't stop them from doing that. However, I can decide how I react to criticism: whether I learn something that helps me grow or ignore it if it contradicts my principles and steady self-esteem.

I am the one who determines whose opinions I value and who genuinely loves me. I analyze their point of view and decide if I want to make changes based on that.

In moments of doubt, I'll remember this: people are evaluating my actions, not my entire personality! Even if they don't always choose the right words. I can change my behavior; it's not set in stone and doesn't define my personality and self-esteem.

For example, my dad keeps saying I'm lazy. It bothers me. Sometimes, I start to doubt myself: "What if he's right?" I know I can work hard on things I'm interested in. I'm fully responsible for my success in school and sports. Sometimes, I just want to relax, but that's not laziness; every person needs some downtime. Is my dad right? What is he really trying to tell me?

STRENGTHENING SELF-ESTEEM

First and foremost, I need to shift my focus from situational self-esteem to steady self-esteem. There are many advantages to steady self-esteem. I'll learn to trust myself, stop doubting my choices, handle life's difficulties, and make decisions on my own. Other people's opinions will bother me less, and I'll feel comfortable with myself. I can strengthen my self-esteem with practice, and there are certain exercises that can help me with that.

I'M A STAR

To start, I'll choose three qualities I like about myself and write them on the inner points of a star. Then, I'll write three qualities I'm not too thrilled about on the outer points. By doing this, I can see that there's room inside the star for both good and not-so-good qualities, yet it still remains a star!

Recognizing and accepting different aspects of my nature will make it easier for me to love and accept myself. And that's where positive change begins.

SELF-TALK

Having negative thoughts about myself can harm my self-esteem. But I can change these thoughts by noticing them and asking, "Is that true? Is that always the case?" Sometimes, simply observing is enough to stop believing in negative thoughts.

I can also replace a negative thought with a positive or neutral one. For example, instead of saying "I never get anything right," I can tell myself, "I make mistakes sometimes, and that's okay."

What do you think about yourself right now? How can you reframe a negative thought about yourself as a positive one?

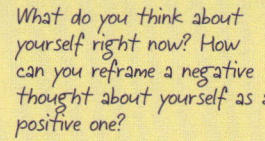

POSITIVE AFFIRMATIONS

These can help me boost my spirits and support myself during tough times.

- I believe in my uniqueness and individuality.
- I acknowledge that I have weaknesses, just like everyone else.
- I recognize and respect my strengths.
- I have a good relationship with myself, as I should.
- I know that I'm okay.
- I'm amazing, I'm love, I'm peace.
- I love myself.

Ego-based self-esteem is always at risk. Self-esteem rooted in the true nature of your inner self is stable and positive.

Unconditional Self-Love

There's nobody closer to me than me. I need my love more than anyone else. But sometimes, I find it hard to fully love myself. I often criticize myself and don't always treat myself kindly. I want to change that. But how?

Loving myself means fully accepting myself, along with my weaknesses and problems. I don't blame myself or punish myself for my mistakes. I learn to live and work with them. I'm always on my side, defending my values and interests. I also see my potential and do what I can to help it flourish. Self-love is a journey toward becoming the best version of myself.

WHAT DOES SELF-LOVE MEAN?

Does loving myself mean indulging in my favorite foods every day, skipping boring classes, and binge-watching TV shows all night long? No.

SELF-LOVE IS ABOUT ACCEPTING MYSELF AND FINDING HARMONY WITHIN MY UNIQUE SELF.

THE FOUNDATION OF MY SELF-LOVE IS BASED ON THESE BELIEFS:

1. My nature is good and my essence is kindness. I always strive for them, even when events in my life bring out my darker side. Bad traits exist within me, just as they do within everyone else, but they're only a small part of me.
2. Everything created by nature is beautiful and deserving of love. I'm a child of nature and deserve love.
3. I, like any living being, am a unique and valuable individual.

Is this true, or do you live by different beliefs? Which ones?

NONE OF THIS IS SELF-LOVE

Is self-love selfishness?
No, because selfishness (in its extreme form) is about ignoring others' needs for the sake of my own. Self-love involves respecting both my interests and those of others.

Is self-love an excuse for weaknesses?
No, because self-love helps me see my potential and inspires me to take the next steps in development.

Is self-love self-pity?
No, because self-pity humiliates me and turns me into a victim. Self-love empowers me to seek a better version of myself.

Self-love has a strategic and systematic nature — I look ahead and choose what's best for me in the grand scheme of life, not just in a specific situation.

How will your life change if you learn to love yourself?

7 PETALS OF SELF-LOVE BY DR. SHAINNA ALI

How developed are these aspects of self-love in you? Ponder this and rate each petal from 1 to 10.

Self-love is beautiful, like a flower. It's the foundation of my relationship with myself and includes seven aspects:

1. **Self-Analysis:** I recognize my thoughts, feelings, and desires, and control my actions.

2. **Self-Understanding:** I understand my true nature and don't fear looking inside myself.

3. **Self-Care:** I know what helps and supports me, and I don't deny it to myself.

4. **Self-Esteem:** I accept my weak and strong sides equally.

5. **Self-Kindness:** I treat myself kindly and benevolently.

6. **Self-Respect:** I understand my worth and don't hesitate to stand up for my interests.

7. **Self-Development:** I constantly seek opportunities to become better.

I will be able to love myself if I…

- Remain a center of attention among my friends.
- Help my parents more often.
- Stay in a good mood all the time…

But why am I setting conditions for myself? I love a cat, for example, just as it is, without expecting it to become a tiger. I love my loved ones simply for existing. So, I deserve love just for being born! Right now, without any conditions, tell yourself, "I love you!"

What conditions for self-love often pop up in your mind?

SELF-LOVE PRACTICE

Self-love, like all important relationships in my life, requires attention and conscious practice. It's a skill that I can and should learn.

6 DAILY SELF-LOVE PRACTICES BY BLAKE BAUER

1. I honestly and kindly express what I feel and what I need.
2. I understand my goals and needs and act accordingly.
3. I make time for activities that bring me joy.
4. I spend time alone as often as I need.
5. I value my time and energy. I say no to what's unimportant, non-prioritized, or harmful.
6. I take care of my body and choose what's healthy for my well-being.

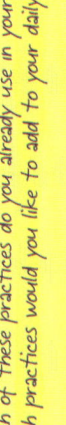

Which of these practices do you already use in your life? Which practices would you like to add to your daily life?

Should I Fear Loneliness?

Loneliness is something we all go through. To me, it feels like an emptiness and like I'm disconnected from the whole world. I might try to avoid it by keeping busy with different activities. Sometimes I wonder why we suffer from being lonely. Maybe it's because our fear of loneliness stops us from understanding it better.

FEELING LONELY? YOU'RE NOT ALONE!

Ever felt lonely? Turns out, pretty much every one of us has been there. According to a study by the BBC that involved 55,000 people worldwide, 40% of people aged 16 to 24 said they feel lonely often or very often.

And it's not just about physical isolation either (though that became more common during the pandemic). What people really struggle with is emotional or psychological loneliness, like feeling lonely even when you're in a group or with your family.

This kind of loneliness occurs when you feel like you:
- Don't belong to a group.
- Don't have someone to share your experiences with.
- Don't get understanding and support from the people around you.

IS LONELINESS A BAD THING?

Loneliness by itself isn't bad or dangerous. How we feel about it is what can make it unpleasant. Loneliness can make us feel sad, helpless, frustrated, angry, or even ashamed.

There are different kinds of loneliness

Ego-Loneliness is when we're lonely because we're too focused on ourselves, competing for attention, trying to get more likes on social media — basically, it's all about feeding our ego.

Self-Loneliness, on the other hand, happens when we're missing something deeper inside ourselves, something we need.

WHY DO TEENS FEEL SO LONELY?

STAGE OF DEVELOPMENT: FITTING IN

At this age, fitting in with a group and being accepted and belonging is extremely important. The BBC study mentioned above found that young people have huge expectations when it comes to friendships — we want to have a lot of friends and connect with them deeply. So, we try to be part of a group, and we have an image to maintain. If we don't follow the group's norms, we might end up feeling lonely or even rejected.

A TIME OF CHANGE AND SELF-DISCOVERY

Being a teenager means lots of changes. We're growing up, figuring out our interests, switching schools, and trying to find our purpose in life. It's like we're painting a picture of ourselves, but it's not finished yet — we're still adding the colors. And as we change, the people around us change too. We might not be as close with certain friends as we used to be, and we might not have become super close with new friends yet. It's not always easy to find our crew, and often they're not the people we see every day. Even our families, who supported us when we were kids, might feel more distant as we become more independent.

HOW LONELINESS AFFECTS OUR RELATIONSHIPS

GOING ALONG WITH THE GROUP

When we feel lonely or don't fit in, it can make us do things we wouldn't normally do just to belong. Sometimes, these things can be risky, like trying drugs or hanging out with a group that does things that are against the law. These extremes are easy to spot, but I've known people who got into trouble simply because they were trying so hard to fit in with a group.

But even smaller changes in ourselves or wearing a mask to blend in with a group can make us lose touch with our real selves. It disconnects us from understanding our true nature and desires. For example, if a group you hang around with likes to gossip and talk behind people's backs, you might start doing it just to fit in. After a while, you might realize you're gossiping out of habit. **Losing ourselves and losing touch with our deep needs is too high a price to pay for a false sense of belonging.**

NIHILISM: "I DON'T NEED ANYONE"

On the other hand, some of us might go to the extreme of thinking we don't need anyone after a bad breakup or rejection. We might suppress our emotions, avoid relationships, and think we're better off alone. This kind of behavior can lead to serious problems like depression and apathy. It's just another way we lose touch with ourselves and our true needs.

SO, WHAT CAN WE DO ABOUT LONELINESS?

1. **First, it's important to accept that feeling lonely is normal.** It's not something to be ashamed of — it's part of being human.

2. **Remember that loneliness is temporary.** Changing your surroundings or your perception of a situation can help ease the feeling.

3. **Don't always believe your thoughts.** Thoughts aren't reality or facts, and they're not who we are. By observing our thoughts from the outside, we can see how they come and go without affecting us. Thoughts about loneliness are just thoughts.

4. **Help people who need support.** There's nothing like genuine gratitude from another person to remind us of our worth.

5. **Reconnect with old friends, and talk to relatives, even those you don't see often.** Sometimes, you'll find interesting people among them.

6. **Explore new places, even if it's just a different part of your town.** Use the summer, vacations, or weekends to get away from your usual social circle and meet new people.

7. **Find your crew.** Don't settle for a group that doesn't feel right for you. Your people might be in a different club or a group of volunteers who share your interests. They might not be your age or even live in your city.

AND NOW, THE OTHER SIDE... YES, THERE'S VALUE IN LONELINESS TOO!

On the other hand, I've come to appreciate moments of solitude and time alone. It helps me stay connected with myself and learn more about my needs, interests, and desires.

— I can think about recent events and what I've learned.
— I write in my journal.
— I draw, play my guitar, and indulge in my creative pursuits.
— I'm learning to meditate, observe myself objectively, and discover new things about myself.
— I spend more time in nature, go for walks, and play with my dog.
— I do things I truly love: reading, cooking, building, repairing things.

Loneliness can help me build a genuine relationship with myself and show me that there's nothing scary about spending time alone doing something that I'm truly interested in.

Being Authentic

We all face moments where we have to decide how to express ourselves — whether in a new group, during a discussion, or even on a date. We wonder if we should conform and blend in or firmly state what truly matters to us. "Just be yourself" is the most common advice we get from parents and friends. But what does that even mean?

WHAT IS AUTHENTICITY, OR BEING YOURSELF?

Authenticity is the ability to honestly and openly express yourself in alignment with your values, needs, and desires.

PSYCHOLOGISTS BRIAN KERNIS AND MICHAEL GOLDMAN IDENTIFY FOUR ELEMENTS OF AUTHENTICITY:

Self-Awareness: Knowing your values, capabilities, aspirations, desires, and emotions and trusting them.

Self-Reflection: Internally analyzing your characteristics and behaviors without denial or guilt.

Behavior: Taking actions that reflect your values and personal needs independently of criticism or others' opinions.

Relationships: Choosing honest and open relationships.

WHY BE AUTHENTIC?

Being yourself isn't an easy path. It demands courage. Sometimes, it causes me to lose relationships because not everyone is ready for such honesty and openness. Sometimes, it makes me go against the crowd. Sometimes, I risk being the odd one out among my peers. Choosing to be myself doesn't mean I think I'm better than others. So why would I want to take on this challenge of being myself if it can be so difficult?

Because it's the only way to live in harmony with ourselves, build true, deep connections, and fully realize our potential. It's only by boldly expressing my inner self that I can fully realize myself and my potential.

Authenticity allows me to make choices based on my desires, even if they're not popular choices. It helps me pick friends who genuinely connect with me and are valuable to me. Authenticity is the foundation of my success and happiness; it's unique to my concept of a fulfilling life.

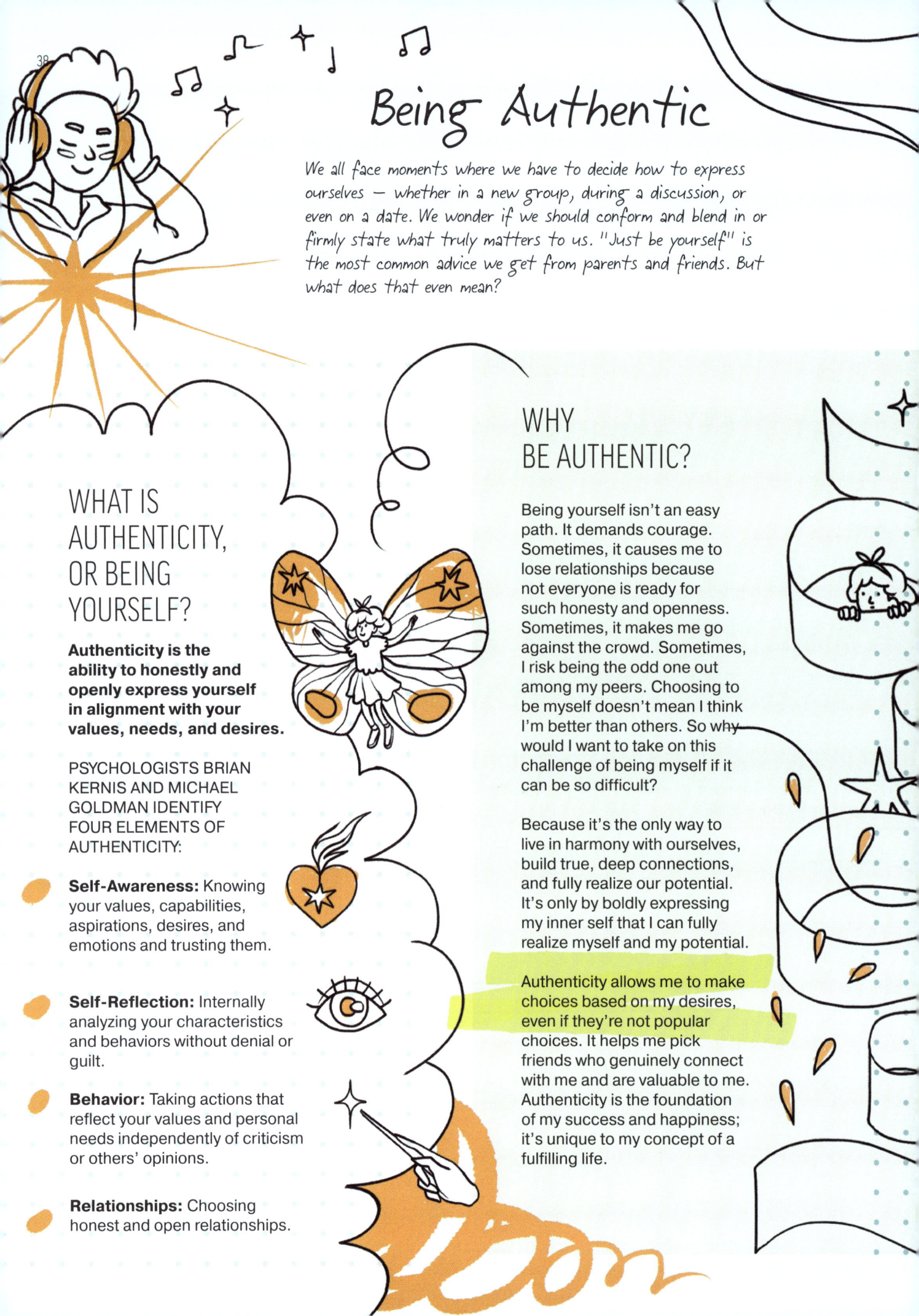

HOW TO RECONNECT WITH YOURSELF

Dr. Gabor Maté, a therapist specializing in trauma and addiction, uses the **Four A's** to help people reconnect with their inner selves:

1. **Authenticity:** I set aside time to consciously understand my desires, intentions, and ambitions, and I allow myself to act on them.

2. **Agency:** I make deliberate decisions and take responsibility for my actions. Agency empowers me to choose who I am and who I want to become. I align with my values and principles, not others' expectations.

3. **Anger:** Anger guards my boundaries. I permit myself to be angry, experience negative emotions, and learn to say no. I express dissatisfaction openly and promptly while caring for the feelings of others.

4. **Acceptance:** I embrace my whole self, acknowledging that everything within me is part of my unique personality. I take pride in myself. I accept the world as it is, recognizing its goodness and worth.

CAN YOU LOSE YOURSELF?

"I" isn't something that can be misplaced in the attic with old junk. It's always inside me, but I can lose my connection with it or with my inner self if I regularly make choices that go against my values and desires.

For instance, I might decide to go see a tutor even though I feel belittled by their teaching style. Each time, my inner self's voice grows quieter and weaker until, one day, I consider the tutor's behavior normal. I will still feel uncomfortable and reluctant about going to my lessons, but I won't be able to explain why.

Trying to please everyone or being unable to say no can also lead to the same result — losing touch with your true needs and desires. What's so bad about that? The consequences include feelings of unfulfillment, unhappiness, depression, and even illness.

HONESTY DOESN'T MEAN RUDENESS

To be honest, you don't have to be brutally blunt. You can express your opinions or preferences directly while maintaining a kind and respectful tone. How? By choosing the right voice, words, and expressions.

What's next?

Take a moment to think:

- How do you feel about yourself? What can you improve in your self-relationship?

- How well do you know yourself? Write down what you value in yourself and in others. What activities and hobbies bring you special joy?

- Do you enjoy spending time alone? Why or why not?

- What can you be proud of about yourself? Write down at least 10 points.

Reading material:

- "The Chemistry of Joy: A Three-Step Program for Overcoming Depression Through Western Science and Eastern Wisdom" by Henry Emmons and Rachel Kranz
- "Breaking the Habit of Being Yourself: How to Lose Your Mind and Create a New One" by Dr. Joe Dispenza
- "Radical Acceptance: Embracing Your Life With the Heart of a Buddha" by Tara Brach

Watch and learn:

Amy Cuddy's TED Talk on **"Your Body Language May Shape Who You Are"**

Susan Cain's TED Talk on **"The Power of Introverts"**

Helen Farrell's TED Talk on **"What Is Depression?"**

CHAPTER 3
Me and My Family

- The Value of Family

- The Rules of a Healthy Family Life

- When Your Family Isn't Perfect

- Is My Adult Family a Clone of My Childhood?

- *What's Next?*

The Value of Family

In the past, people leaned on each other because living together meant safety (one person would handle the homestead, while the other would protect it from potential dangers) and made economic sense (multiple generations shared one house). But in our modern world, there aren't as many immediate physical threats that you need to be shielded from, and most people can afford to maintain their own households. So, why do we still live together as families?

Family fulfills a fundamental human need — a sense of belonging and emotional connection.

In a world that encourages individualism, where everyone insists on his or her own personal space, it can be challenging to recognize that our happiness is closely tied to our connections and reliance on one another. Perhaps the failure to grasp this concept is what is causing so many people today to struggle with feelings of loneliness, depression, and anxiety.

Emotional attachment serves as the cornerstone of family dynamics. Different types of attachment can exist within a family:

SECURE ATTACHMENT

In these families, members consistently offer emotional support and feel close to one another. They live with the belief that most people are good, trust others easily, make new friends effortlessly, and take pleasure in life.

ANXIOUS ATTACHMENT

In these families, members sometimes receive support from one another. They often feel like the world doesn't notice them and view themselves as unimportant. To get attention or earn love, they believe they must do something extraordinary.

AVOIDANT ATTACHMENT

Family members doubt they will receive attention even if they cry out. They don't feel a connection with their close relatives and tend to avoid contact. This type of attachment often leads to unreliable relationships that require significant effort to change.

DISMISSIVE ATTACHMENT

Members of families with dismissive attachment refuse to acknowledge each other's needs and may hurt or insult one another, occasionally resorting to physical violence. They often perceive the world as a threat. This is a destructive form of attachment.

So, what type of attachment thrives in a happy family? What type of attachment exists in your family?

Any family member can initiate a shift in the family's attachment style by consciously choosing to communicate differently, while remaining grounded in love. Politeness, care, and attention are contagious. Gradually, step by step, others will join in.

To build a strong attachment within your family you need:

RESPECT

Rudeness, impoliteness, dishonesty, or humiliation indicate a lack of respect within the family. Everyone, regardless of age, deserves equal respect.

A SENSE OF VALUE

Excessive protection, constant rejection, a lack of boundaries, permissiveness ("she's still young"), inattentiveness, and not knowing how to listen can harm a person's sense of self-worth.

ACCEPTANCE

Suppressing emotions, demanding perfection, focusing on negative feedback, and constant reprimands can hinder acceptance. On the other hand, secure attachment arises when family members express gratitude, acknowledge positive qualities, and celebrate each other's successes.

BELONGING

A sense of connection to other family members grows stronger through shared traditions, activities like family game nights, family meetings, and making significant decisions together, such as discussing trips, changing residences, or job choices.

SAFETY

Physical and emotional abuse, strict or unclear boundaries and demands, aggression, and ongoing parental conflicts create a feeling of instability and danger within a family.

Where does this family attachment come from?

Family interactions are heavily influenced by the attachment styles formed by the adult family members during their childhoods. Your parents, often unknowingly, shape your attachment style, which you carry with you throughout your life.

The Rules of a Healthy Family Life

The great Leo Tolstoy once said, "All happy families are alike…" He wasn't too far from the truth. So, what are the characteristics of a healthy family?

Unconditional Value of the Individual

The most significant difference in a healthy, or functional, family is that it exists for the people within it. The importance of each person and the sense of belonging are its core values. In a healthy family, everyone strives to make life better for each other.

Stability and Growth

A healthy family provides its members with a sense of stability. Life within the family is predictable and understandable. You can anticipate how the family and its members will react to events or actions, giving you a firm footing no matter what happens. However, if a family becomes overly focused on stability, any change can lead to crises, stress, and conflicts.

That's why a functional family also possesses flexibility and the ability to adapt. Since families are constantly changing — children grow up, become independent, and eventually leave the nest, adults age, people get sick, and some may pass away — support in accepting change and adapting to it is part of a healthy family's work.

Closed and Open Boundaries

In a healthy family, there's a dual task. On one hand, a family is an intimate circle where outsiders are not readily invited. Not every new friend will be welcomed to a family gathering. Families protect themselves and their norms from hostile intrusion, establishing external boundaries. On the other hand, these boundaries are more like sheer curtains, allowing information from the external environment to filter through. They can expand to welcome new family members, fostering growth and development.

Hierarchy and Freedom

In a healthy family, there's no doubt about who to turn to for help or advice. It's clear whom you can rely on. This might be a single person, the family head, or several adults who share responsibilities.

However, adults in a healthy family don't misuse their positions. They involve other family members in decision-making, grant them the freedom to act according to their judgment, and avoid stifling them with rigid "you can't do that" constraints. The level of independence and responsibility given to children in the family increases as they grow older.

Emotions

In a healthy family, like any other, people experience emotions. They argue and make up, get angry and feel hurt, rejoice and get sad. The key difference is that emotions can be shared without shame, expressed openly, and discussed without being considered a weakness or something shameful. On the other hand, emotions don't overwhelm family members, becoming an uncontrollable hurricane that destroys relationships.

In the past, ideal families were believed to be devoid of negative emotions. Individuals from such families tended to hide their feelings. Humanity is only beginning to learn how to live in a world where emotions are accepted as part of human nature.

What is the relationship with emotions like in your family?

Roles

Family life is rich with roles. For example, "adult" or "child," "peacemaker" or "rebel." Roles often develop spontaneously based on circumstances and individual tendencies. However, they can also be designated by agreement. For instance, you might decide to be the "treasurer," excelling at managing finances and keeping track of the family budget. Having a role makes family members feel important and valued contributors to family life.

But remember, people and their needs are more important than roles! Even if you have a role, you have the right to decline or change it. In a healthy system, a role doesn't consume the person. You can step down or switch roles when necessary.

Rules

We say good morning. We don't arrive late. We invite guests into our home. These are examples of rules that have developed within families. Some are explicit, while others are unspoken but have formed through repetition and tradition. Rules exist to ensure that family members live together comfortably and predictably. They foster a sense of belonging but should never stifle personal freedom and authenticity.

In healthy families, people communicate openly. They discuss not only practical matters like "Take out the trash" or "What's for dinner?" but also share their day, special events, difficulties, and victories. They engage in philosophical and psychological discussions, allowing everyone to have their own opinion.

What rules exist in your family?
Are there any that you disagree with or find challenging to follow?

When Your Family Isn't Perfect

A family can come in all shapes and sizes. It might have two or twenty people. They might be young or old, married or single, or they may or may not be related by blood. What matters is whether everyone in the family wants to be together. But let's face it, that isn't always easy.

A Place to Learn

You can't find a perfect family because every family is made up of regular people who have their flaws. No matter how unique your family might be, it's a place where you learn some important stuff, such as to accept others, how to love and take care of them, how to build relationships, and how to figure out who you are. Think of it as a safe place to practice important life skills. For example, it's easier to learn how to say no when you're saying it to your mom or dad because they're usually good at understanding your needs.

Divorced Parents — Is It Still a Family?

Divorce can be tough for a family. Things change, and it might seem like the family you knew doesn't exist anymore. But if the key part is still there — like love and relationships — then your family still exists, even if it looks a bit different. It's crucial to maintain these connections and relationships with both of your parents and not get stuck in the past, which can't be changed.

My Parents Are Always Busy. We Only Talk About My School and Chores. Do They Even Care About Me?

Chances are, your parents have lost sight of what's really important to them. This happens a lot when they get caught up in all the different things that seem urgent to them. They work and make money, thinking they're taking care of the family and securing a good present and future for you. But this idea of providing for the family often takes the place of why they started a family and had you in the first place. In this situation, it's important to talk to your parents about what you feel and need (but do it kindly). Don't be afraid to remind them that their attention is very important to you and you want to communicate more. You can even invite them on a regular recurring date, either all of you or one-on-one.

Why Do They Control Me? I'm Not a Little Kid Anymore!

Some parents find it hard to see their child as an adult and treat them that way. It's not easy for everyone to adjust to changes. Others might show their care by trying to control things, like saying, "Did you remember your hat?" To show that you can be independent and responsible, you can:

1. Take on a task and do it regularly (make sure your parents are aware of it).
2. Decide which responsibilities you're going to handle together with your parents.
3. Gradually take on more tasks as they trust you. It's important to talk about your achievements and willingness to take on more.

To prove you deserve this freedom, you shouldn't create a big fuss or start a revolution — that'll only make them see you as a kid.

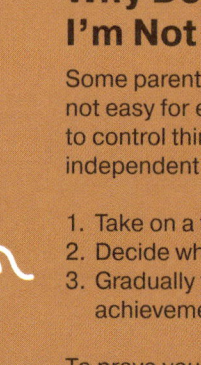

Is It Okay to Get Angry at My Parents?

Feeling any emotion is normal. It's likely that in your family, it's common to hide anger, and it might even be seen as something bad. But the sooner you talk about what's bothering you, the less intense your anger will be. It might start as just a little annoyance, but if you keep it to yourself, it can fester and grow into a huge outburst of rage. Anger can actually be helpful because it gives you the energy to protect your boundaries. So go ahead and constructively express your anger and find your own way to talk to your parents about it.

How Can I Talk to My Parents So They'll Listen?

Do you listen to them? We often expect others to change first when we can make the first move ourselves. Communication goes both ways. Try taking that first step toward them, and they'll probably follow. If they don't, then you'll have more reason to ask for respect and negotiate how you communicate.

Why Do My Siblings Even Exist?

Your brothers and sisters are your best teachers for life and how to deal with people your age. They teach you how to stand up for yourself, protect yourself and others, forgive, reach agreements, work together, and lead. Siblings are like your support system and they will be your family once your parents aren't around.

How Can I Forgive My Parents for Hurtful Things from the Past?

Here are some tips from psychologist Lyudmila Petranovskaya:

- **Try to understand** that your parents might have grown up in families where they were hurt. They might not have had much experience or maybe their lives are tough right now, leaving them with little room for proper communication.
- **Don't keep things to yourself.** Talk about your feelings and things that hurt you without blaming them.
- **Ask** your parents to take responsibility for what they did or for a situation that hurt you.
- **Don't expect** your parents to change overnight.
- **Allow yourself to feel sad.** Some things were missing or weren't right in your childhood, and they'll never come back. It's sad, but you can still have a good life.
- **Feel sorry for your childhood self.** Be the adult who supports and takes care of them.
- **Don't hold onto your past traumas and grudges forever.** Let go of them and create a new story about yourself that isn't limited by the past.

Is My Adult Family a Clone of My Childhood?

We might inherit a good family or a bad one. The type of adult family we will have depends on whether we can change the behaviors we learned from our parents' family. So, what kind of changes are we talking about?

Choosing Through Family Lenses

Subconsciously, we tend to seek a partner who fits our family's mold: someone who shares its traits or complements what's missing. Even through nonverbal signals, we read the emotional baggage and behavior of someone we're interested in and measure them against our family norms. However, this process shouldn't remain unconscious. On the contrary, the better we understand the peculiarities of our parents' family, the easier it will be to modify our legacy to match what we want to see in our family.

Stages of Development and the Family's Role

Each child goes through several crucial stages of development, and the family plays a significant role in them. If a stage isn't completed for some reason, adults may struggle with fears, limitations, insecurities, or unrealistic expectations. Family therapist Robin Skynner identifies 5 stages:

To be sure, unfinished stages of development aren't a life sentence. You can get through them at any age by understanding what skills you lack. Often, people do this intuitively, but it's easier with the support of a psychologist.

3 INFLUENCE OF SIBLINGS AND FRIENDS

Age 3 to 10 is the time when social skills are formed, including how to cooperate, compete, defend oneself, compromise, make friends, and share. Skipping this stage can lead to indecisiveness, an inability to assert one's boundaries, or inflexibility and a tendency to press others.

1 THE MOTHER'S INFLUENCE

Until around 2-3 years old, it's a time of unconditional love and care. A lack of attention and warmth from the mother makes it difficult for an adult to build close relationships, care for others, or express love.

4 INFLUENCE OF THE GENDER INTEREST

From 12 years old onwards, it's time to develop romantic relationships, as you start to understand the behavior of all sexes, norms for showing romantic and sexual interest, and the emergence of empathy in relationships.

2 THE FATHER'S INFLUENCE

At around 3 years old, the first signs of independence and self-reliance appear. Clear rules and control are needed. Without completing this stage, a person may have problems with self-discipline.

5 SEPARATION FROM THE FAMILY

From 12 years old onwards, you experience the period of independence from your parents. It teaches you independence, responsibility. Unresolved separation issues can make it difficult to build equal partner relationships.

Attachment Styles

Adult partners often display the attachment style that they developed during their childhood with their parents. A partner with an anxious or avoidant attachment style tends to focus on their own feelings and needs. People with a secure attachment style balance attention between themselves and their partner. People with different attachment styles often speak contrasting emotional languages. If we consciously comprehend what's happening in our relationships, we can change our attachment style.

Emotional Baggage

The accepted norms in our family determine how we express our emotions. "Don't get angry. Don't whine. Emotions are for the weak. Boys don't cry. Girls should be obedient." Sound familiar? Similar patterns exist in many families. So, what should we do with emotions that were forbidden or unwanted at home? By suppressing and denying them, we pile them up in a big chest that we carry throughout our lives.

When choosing a partner, we subconsciously expect their chest to contain similar contents. We think they'll express their emotions just like in our own family. Or, wanting to free ourselves from the burden of our emotional baggage, we seek a partner who freely expresses the emotions we've hidden.

Either way, there's a moment when the contents of the chest explode due to tension, which can damage the relationship. To avoid this, it's essential to consciously open the chest, sort through it, discuss what's hidden, and agree on the rules for expressing emotions in a new relationship. In a stable relationship, people are willing to change, accept criticism, and evolve together.

What Kind of Family Do I Want?

Analyzing your parents' family and sketching the blueprint for the family you want to build helps you prepare for the right choice. It allows you to recognize patterns and understand what constitutes unacceptable behavior. Start drawing the ideal picture of your family, so that when the time comes to make decisions, you already have a complete vision.

What's next?

Take a moment to think:

- Make a list of 10 habits that you've inherited from your family. Which ones do you like? Which ones do you want to get rid of?

- What can you thank your parents for? Take the time to express your gratitude.

- In what ways do you resemble your parents? What are some of their qualities or traits that you would like to emulate?

Reading material:

- "Boundaries: When to Say Yes, When to Say No to Take Control of Your Life" by Dr. Henry Cloud and Dr. John Townsend

- "Listening: The Forgotten Skill" by Madelyn Burley-Allen

- "Daughter Detox: Recovering from an Unloving Mother and Reclaiming Your Life" by Peg Streep

Watch and learn:

Elizabeth Zion's TED Talk
on **"The Need for Family Reunification to Make Families Whole Again"**

Julian Treasure's TED Talk
on **"5 Ways to Listen Better"**

CHAPTER 4
Me and My Friends

The Importance of Friendship

Friends are our support system. Through our interactions with them, we figure out boundaries, learn to understand people's feelings, and build up trust in the world. However, not all friendships can make us happier.

Why Do We Need Friends?

Friendship helps us grow: it teaches us to negotiate and work as a team. With the help of our friends, we achieve our goals faster and feel happier. Moreover, friendship is a powerful source of positive energy. Sometimes, a few kind words from a friend can turn a bad day into a good one.

What Does Friendship Mean?

Friendship is a strong connection that's built on mutual support, trust, respect, and acceptance.

IN A HEALTHY FRIENDSHIP, THE KEY VALUES FOR YOU AND YOUR FRIEND ARE:

DEEP KNOWLEDGE OF ONE ANOTHER

- Want to get to know each other better.
- Spend a lot of time together.
- Share common interests.
- Work on the relationship and make up after arguments.
- Discuss relationship difficulties instead of keeping them quiet.

EQUAL CONTRIBUTION

- Invest in the relationship equally.

RESPECT

- Avoid doing things that would upset each other.
- Look for activities that both of you enjoy, rather than insisting on your preferences.
- Respect differences rather than trying to change each other.

SUPPORT

- Help each other overcome difficulties.
- Compliment each other.
- Don't compete against one another, but celebrate each other's successes.

ACCEPTANCE

- Love one another for who you are.
- Accept each other's flaws and find beauty in your imperfections.

TRUST

- Feel comfortable sharing secrets and know they'll be kept safe.
- Feel at ease and secure when you're together.
- Share your feelings, thoughts, and ideas openly.

Friendship for Survival

For a long time, people believed that friendship was their own invention, but it turns out it's a gift from evolution. Close social bonds helped our ancestors stay alive: it was much easier for them to find food and protect themselves from danger when they were in groups. Even today, friendship plays a crucial role in the lives of all social animals, from monkeys to dolphins. Being around friends makes them (just like us) live longer, recover from difficulties faster, and feel less stressed.

Being on the Same Level

Friendship is our first experience with a relationship on equal terms. In a family, we're often in the role of a subordinate: we listen to adults and depend on them. With friends, we can just be ourselves without feeling superior or inferior. Equality is the foundation of friendship. Yet, it's not about keeping score — "I give you as much as you give me." Equality means that you and your friend both get exactly what you need from the relationship.

Riding a Seesaw

Friendship is like a seesaw: for it to move, both of you have to make an effort. When one of you gets attention, you are lifted up, and then you help lift your friend up in return.

Sometimes, there can be an imbalance in a friendship. One of you might invest more time, energy, or attention and get less in return. It might feel like one of you is firmly on the ground while the other is up in the air, and the seesaw isn't moving.

To fix this imbalance, ask your friend: "Are you getting everything you need from our friendship? Is there anything else I can do for you?"

If you're the one who feels like you're not getting enough, talk to your friend about it gently. A simple approach might help:

say something nice + **express your feelings** + **make a request**

For example: "I enjoy spending time with you, but sometimes, I feel sad when you make all the decisions about where we go. Can we decide together next time?"

Loneliness Is Not the Answer

Sometimes, building and maintaining relationships is challenging. You might even think that life would be easier without friends. However, evolution disagrees: the human body sees loneliness as a threat. Prolonged loneliness can be very stressful for our brains. Of course, this doesn't mean you should befriend just anyone, as unhealthy relationships can be even worse.

Close Friendship

Aristotle, the famous philosopher, once said that true friendship is when we share values and interests with others. In today's world, we call this type of friendship "close friendship." Sounds great, but how do we build it?

You Can't Have Too Many Best Friends

Researcher Jeff Hall found that it takes about 40-60 hours of interaction to go from strangers to friends. It takes around 80 to 100 hours to consider someone a friend and more than 200 hours for someone to become your best friend. On average, most people have 2-3 close friends they deeply connect with.

What's important is how you spend your time together. Do you talk about your feelings? Do you consider your friend's life as important as your own and prioritize your friendship?

The Friendship Scale

How many friends do you think of as close friends? Put them on this scale below and see if it matches your feelings:

CASUAL ACQUAINTANCES: You discuss everyday life and share opinions on things that don't matter much.

FRIENDS: You share your goals and values, but don't get emotionally involved or, on the contrary, talk emotionally about abstract topics. You share your achievements with each other.

GOOD FRIENDS: You talk about personal events and feelings, including negative ones. You're willing to share things that others might judge you for.

CLOSE FRIENDS: You talk about your relationship (e.g., "I miss you" or "I enjoy spending time with you"). You share what moves you. You're not afraid.

BEST FRIENDS: You strive to be closer to each other. You express love and care. You're willing to work on the relationship. You're not afraid to share embarrassing stories or things others don't know.

Vulnerability Is the Key

To have a close friendship, you've got to be open and vulnerable. That means letting people see the real you, even during awkward moments. Vulnerability is like a warm, comforting hug, but to experience it, you need to break down the walls of shame and fear.

It's Not a Weakness

We all have our vulnerable side, but we often hide it because we think it's a sign of weakness. The truth is, being vulnerable is a sign of great strength. Imagine how brave it is to open up to someone and say "You mean a lot to me" without knowing if they'll say it back.

Psychologist Brené Brown believes that the "culture of never enough" makes us hide our true selves. Society often measures a person by their achievements. When we always feel pressure to be perfect, we start to think of ourselves as failures, close ourselves off from people, and feel ashamed.

Being Vulnerable

By being vulnerable, we learn to trust those close to us and give them the opportunity to trust and open up to us. To be vulnerable means:

 embracing imperfection ("I'm having a tough time and feel like crying, and that's perfectly okay");

handling uncertainty ("I'm unsure how my friend will respond to my tears");

 taking an emotional risk ("but I won't hold back");

feeling whole no matter what happens ("any response won't shake me; I'll keep believing that I'm okay").

Shame

Shame is the main obstacle to vulnerability. It's different from guilt. Guilt is related to our actions. It helps us acknowledge mistakes and fix them. Shame, on the other hand, tears us apart and prevents us from seeing our basic goodness.

Behind shame is the fear of losing relationships. We're scared that if we open up, people will see our flaws and leave. The "culture of never enough" tells us that only a select few are worthy of love. But, in reality, love is given to those who accept and love themselves and others, imperfections and all.

We are all imperfect, yet good enough and deserving of love just as we are. Understanding this is the key to letting yourself be vulnerable and building true friendships.

Learning to Be Vulnerable

Build Resilience to Shame: Create a list of things you like about yourself and read it when you feel ashamed.

Replace Shame with Compassion: Don't be too hard on yourself or others for mistakes; be kind and understanding. Say, "Everyone makes mistakes; it's just part of life. I'm not perfect, and that's okay."

Conquer Your Fears: Try doing the opposite of what scares you — share your feelings without thinking about how others will react.

See the Beauty in Imperfection: Just like you can love a tree despite its crooked branches, you can love a person despite their flaws.

What Are Boundaries?

Each person has their own "personal space bubble" — boundaries that define where they feel comfortable in their interactions. The better you understand your own and others' boundaries, the easier it is to communicate comfortably.

How to Recognize When Your Boundaries Have Been Crossed

Try a little exercise called "The Space Test." Ask a friend to stand about six feet away from you and take one step towards you every 30 seconds. After each step, ask yourself when you start feeling a bit uncomfortable, and pinpoint the moment you wish they'd take a step back.

Remember these sensations. Chances are, this is how you feel when any of your boundaries are crossed, not just your physical ones.

Your Rules

Personal boundaries are the rules you set to keep your inner peace intact. Essentially, these are guidelines you establish to ensure that your communication is safe and comfortable.

BOUNDARIES MIGHT BE:
- **Physical:** protect your body, personal belongings, and personal space.
- **Psychological:** guard your time, emotions, decisions, and values.

OTHER SIGNS THAT YOUR BOUNDARIES MIGHT HAVE BEEN CROSSED INCLUDE:
- Feeling irritation, annoyance, guilt, or shame.
- Convincing yourself with phrases like, "Maybe I should help, what's the harm?" "I'll tough it out," "It's awkward to say no," or "I don't want people thinking I'm a bad person."

BOTH TYPES OF BOUNDARIES MAY BE:

FIRM
These are **"NO" boundaries,** things that are absolutely unacceptable in your interactions. For example, it's **unacceptable** to resort to violence or insult you.

SOFT
These are **"PLEASE DON'T" boundaries,** or things that you'd rather avoid. Most boundaries are flexible, and they can change depending on the people and situations involved. For example, you might tell one friend, **"Please don't** criticize me," but ask another for feedback. For example: **"Please, don't** discuss me behind my back or raise your voice at me."

What is unacceptable for you? What do you prefer to avoid? Take a moment to think about your own "NO" and "PLEASE DON'T" lists for how you interact with a close friend.

What to Do to Protect Yourself

1. Share your two lists of rules, "NO" and "PLEASE DON'T," with your friend and suggest they create their own.

2. If someone crosses your boundaries, gently let them know. You can use a simple format: "I feel + when you do + because + so please." For example: "I feel uneasy when you judge my appearance because how I look reflects my idea of beauty. So please, let's not judge me anymore."

3. Be patient; it might take a few conversations to make your boundaries clear. Give your friend the right to make a mistake.

4. Warn them about the consequences. If your friend disrespects your boundaries for a third time, add an "or else" clause (for firm boundaries, you can add this after the second violation). For instance: "Don't do that again, or else I'll have to leave, and we'll stop hanging out." The "or else" part can be anything, as long as you're willing to follow through. Don't make promises you won't keep.

Protecting your boundaries isn't about trying to change or punish people. Your boundaries are all about your emotions, body, and values.

For example, saying, "You can't force me to talk if I don't want to" is about how others should interact with you. However, the statement, "If we're friends, you can't hang out with anyone else" is an attempt to control someone else's actions and disregard their boundaries. See the difference?

The best way to respect other people's boundaries is to ask. "Is it okay if I give you a hug?" or "Do you need my advice?" It's crucial to accept their response, whether it's a yes or no, without needing an explanation.

DISREGARDING OTHER PEOPLE'S BOUNDARIES INVOLVES...

...shaming, humiliating, insulting, lying, not keeping promises, pressuring, making decisions for others, speaking for them, forcing, giving unsolicited advice, demanding, accusing, manipulating, coercing, ignoring the person and their feelings, making fun of them, hitting, taking things without asking, disregarding a clear "no," threatening, punishing, or labeling.

Have you ever noticed yourself or your friends doing any of these things?

Friendships and the Obstacles They Face

Even a sturdy ship can be smashed to pieces when it crashes into a solid rock, especially if the crew doesn't see it coming. Friendship works similarly: it's crucial to steer clear of these rocky obstacles. Can you spot them?

Dishonesty

It may sound weird, but we usually don't lie to wreck our friendships; we often do it to protect them. We lie out of a fear of conflict, hurting someone's feelings, or letting them down. While lying may seem helpful in the moment, it usually comes at a steep cost, as we lose trust and, over time, the friendship itself.

How to maintain an honest friendship:

1. **Realize why you're lying in the first place.** For example, if you can't hang out with a friend because you've got other plans, and you lie about going to the doctor, it's to spare their feelings.

2. **Figure out how to be honest about your choice.** Try this formula:

   Regret + Truth + Feelings + Suggestion

   For example: "I'm sorry, but I can't hang out today because I already promised Anna to catch a movie. But I'm happy you invited me. Maybe we can meet up tomorrow?"

3. **Remind yourself of the consequences of deceit;** trust is tough to rebuild.

4. **Don't make promises if you're even slightly unsure.** Take a break and weigh your options.

5. **If you couldn't avoid a lie this time, own up to it later.** Tell your friend you struggle with honesty, but that you're working on it.

Competition

If you and your friend seem locked in a never-ending race, the best thing you can do is stop. Suggest to your friend that you start working together. By cooperating, you can achieve more and better handle any challenges that arise. For instance, you can compete to see who can master coding better. But it's better if you swap tips and double your knowledge and skills.

To stop competing, it's vital to stop comparing yourself to others:

Understand your desires. If you envy someone's success, ask yourself, "Is this truly something that interests me? Will I be better and happier if I achieve the same thing?" If not, let go of trying to catch them and focus on what you love.

Turn the person you envy into a mentor. Ask them to share their experience. This way, you'll focus on your progress, not theirs.

The Quest for Popularity

Wanting to be liked by everyone all the time is an unrealistic goal. Plus, an excessive desire for popularity can make close relationships impossible. Trying to fit in often means living behind a mask. It's hard to keep a close friendship if you're not being genuine with one another.

To keep your friendships, make them a priority:

- **Be there for your friend** during important and tough times.
- **Don't boost your self-esteem at your friend's expense.** Avoid making jokes about them to get laughs from others.
- **Stand up for your friends if they're being mistreated or ignored.** Support their views when others dismiss them.
- **Avoid hypocrisy.** Saying one thing to your friend's face and another in a group chips away at trust and makes your friends wonder if you're talking about them behind their backs.
- **Avoid gossiping.** Spreading rumors creates a destructive pattern in your behavior and makes your friends wonder if you're gossiping about them.
- **Keep secrets.** Avoid sharing any personal details about your friend's life unless you get permission to tell them to someone close to you.

Violence

A breach of boundaries, physical violence, and pressure all ruin friendships. But there are less obvious, yet equally harmful forms of violence, such as belittling, condemning, and accusing. To get rid of these behaviors, use non-violent communication principles:

- **Ask and suggest instead of demanding.** Express your feelings and needs directly instead of making accusations. Use "I" statements (I feel, because/when).
- **Avoid starting a sentence with "no"** as it devalues what comes next.
- **Avoid excessive judgment.** Instead of saying something is "good" or "bad," consider that there might be different viewpoints.
- **Avoid generalizations,** such as "always," "never," "everything," or "nothing."
- **Replace condemnation with understanding.** Offer help instead of unsolicited criticism.

Betrayal

In the broader sense, betrayal is an action that breaches trust and shared values. To avoid betrayal, define what it means for you in advance. Leaving a friend alone in a tough situation is a typical example of betrayal.

WHAT TO DO IF YOU'VE BEEN BETRAYED:

Give yourself time to process the grief. Betrayal is a real loss.
Don't rush to judge; try to understand why it happened. Did your friends realize they were hurting you? Was this a one-time thing or part of a pattern?
List the pros and cons of your relationship.
Decide if you can and want to trust your friends again and forgive them. You're not obligated to. But don't let pride or ego stop you from making a well-thought-out decision.

WHAT NOT TO DO:

Don't stay in a relationship out of fear of loneliness. This prevents you from experiencing genuine friendships, which you deserve.

Finding, Nurturing, and Letting Go

How do you make friends? What do you do to keep friendships alive? How do you navigate ending friendships that have run their course?

How to Make Friends

1. Connect at places that have things you're interested in, such as a concert by your favorite band or a fan meetup. This boosts your odds of meeting someone who shares your interests.

2. When you meet new people casually, try to dig deeper by asking questions about them and what they're passionate about.

3. Try new things; it expands your social circle.

4. Avoid common thinking mistakes that can hold you back when searching for friends.

Here are typical mental hurdles to watch out for:

CATASTROPHIZING: "If I suggest we hang out, they'll laugh at me in front of everyone." **What to do:** Imagine your failure in detail. Is it as terrible as it seems? Give it a shot, as positive or neutral outcomes are more likely.

FORTUNE-TELLING: "She'll think I'm weird because I talk slowly; she won't like me." **What to do:** Remind yourself that no one can predict the future, and life is full of surprises. Don't overthink what others might feel, think, or say.

PROCRASTINATION: "I'll approach them someday, but first, I need to… (fill in the blank)." **What to do:** Start taking action now. No one expects us to be perfect. Everyone is on the lookout for friends. The best time to try is right now.

5. Embrace your failures and rejections as part of the journey.

Which of these approaches are you already using to make friends? What do you find particularly challenging?

What Strengthens Friendship?

THE ABILITY TO COMPROMISE: When you and your friend can easily find win-win solutions and align your needs (your desire to be outdoors + your friend's need for quiet = a picnic in the countryside), you can handle nearly any conflict.

Yet sometimes, it's smart to concede some things. For example, if you really don't like it when people are late, but your friend is chronically tardy, and you know they genuinely respect your boundaries and make an effort to be on time, consider letting that one slide.

SUPPORT: You show your love by being there for your friends during their tough times.

- **Show empathy and offer help** ("What happened is awful. Can I help in any way?").
- **Do exactly what they ask for.** Don't overwhelm your friend with conversations when they need solitude.
- **When your friend confides in you, don't shift the focus onto yourself unless they ask about your experiences.** Express understanding instead ("I can imagine how tough this must be for you").

However, remember that you aren't obligated to solve all your friends' problems. If your friend often has struggles, and their issues persist, gently suggest they consider seeking help from a therapist or mentor.

THE ABILITY TO APOLOGIZE AND MAKE AMENDS: This skill literally saves relationships. Here's how to get better at apologizing:

- Understand what you're apologizing for by carefully listening to your friend.
- Apologize for a specific action. "I won't do it again" sounds insincere.
- Don't make excuses or shift blame.
- Ask how you can make things right and genuinely make an effort to do so.
- Accept any response, even if it means not being forgiven (unfortunately, that might happen).

Saying Goodbye to Friends

Sometimes friendships come to an end. It could be due to a growing misunderstanding, or simply because you've both outgrown the relationship. In any case, parting ways should be done with respect, both for your friend and the shared experiences.

OPTION 1: Open Conversation
- Before saying goodbye, have a heart-to-heart with your friend. Are you sure you can't work things out together? Maybe it's worth a shot.
- If you can't resolve your issues, gently let your friend know it's time to end the friendship. For example, follow this pattern: emotions + reason + the value of your shared history + suggesting parting ways ("It hurts me that every time we meet, we argue and can't see eye to eye. Though I cherish our past friendship, I suggest we end it now before we become outright enemies").
- Allow your friend to express themselves. Show empathy, but don't change your decision out of pity or pressure.
- Establish boundaries: decide if you'll continue to interact with your former friend in group settings or if you prefer not to see them anymore.

OPTION 2: Fading Away
Gradually reduce communication until it naturally stops. Use this method in situations where:

- You believe an honest conversation would be unproductive and could potentially escalate into a bigger conflict. Maybe it's best to put it off until both of you have cooled down and can talk calmly.
- Both of you have lost interest in the friendship, and your friend seems to passively support less contact.

Maintaining Friendships Online

In today's world, friendship isn't limited by distance or the need to hang out in person. You don't have to say goodbye to a close friend forever just because you both move to different cities. Thanks to technology, we can maintain strong friendships online. All you need is the Internet, a shared desire to stay connected, and a bit of know-how about the online world.

How to Maintain Close Friendships at a Distance

Get creative! Think of ways to spend time together, even when you're apart. For example, set up a call and chat while taking a walk outside — it's like a virtual hangout!

Challenges of Online Communication

Social media can be a bit tricky because it doesn't convey nonverbal cues well, making it harder to pick up on your friend's emotions. It's easier to miss signs that they might be irritated or upset. Plus, spending too much time online can sometimes make you feel a bit lonely and disconnected from the real world.

If your friend lives nearby, it's a good idea to hang out in person more often. Try to share your feelings and experiences when you meet face-to-face or, at the very least, through phone calls. And remember, it's best to avoid getting into or continuing arguments online. When we can't see or hear each other, it's easy to make assumptions and draw conclusions based on our own ideas, which may or may not be misguided.

WHEN IT COMES TO DISAGREEMENTS, HERE'S HOW TO HANDLE THEM

 **Slow down** if you find yourself responding to messages quickly without thinking. Suggest to your friend that both of you take a break and continue the conversation when both of you have calmed down.

 Fact-check. If your friend suddenly stops responding during an argument, don't jump to conclusions like, "Why did she leave without listening to me? Doesn't she care about my feelings?" Before sending an angry message:

○ **Separate facts from interpretation.** Fact: your friend is offline, and she's not responding. Interpretation: she left the conversation because she doesn't care.

○ **Consider other possible explanations for what's happening.** Maybe your friend needed a break and will be back soon, or their phone died.

○ **Avoid jumping to conclusions or making impulsive decisions.** Wait for your friend to come back, and ask them what happened.

○ **It's better to talk through disagreements on the phone or through video calls.** This way, you'll get extra information through body language and tone of voice, which helps with understanding.

What Else Takes a Hit When Communicating Online:

○ **Physical closeness:** It's not easy to support a friend without the ability to hug them or be physically present.

○ **Understanding:** Without seeing each other, it's harder to grasp the true meaning of what's being said and the hidden subtext, making it easier to accidentally say something that might be hurtful.

○ **The sense of friendship:** When you're communicating from a distance, it's easy to drift apart and forget about each other.

○ **Safety and trust:** When meeting and interacting online, it's difficult to know whether someone is being truthful about themselves or if they're exaggerating.

 **TIME AND ATTENTION ARE CRUCIAL**

When you and your friend live close by, you naturally spend time together. Try to maintain that same level of regular contact online:

○ **Be there for each other:** make an effort to connect every day. If daily communication is challenging, agree on less frequent calls or messages, like once a week. If you don't chat often, plan for longer conversations when you do.

○ **Make an effort to be present during important moments in each other's lives.** If you accomplish something you've been working hard for, drop your online friend a message like, "Guess what? I did it!"

○ **Balance deep conversations with fun stuff (memes, silly selfies).** Deep talks keep you connected, while lighthearted moments keep things fun.

○ **Try different ways to communicate — find what works for you both.** Everyone's different: some people love long emails, while others prefer video calls. Some set a specific time to be online together, while others exchange messages throughout the day.

○ **Build that sense of "we" — the feeling of being a team.** Help each other out, share your interests (for example, combine your hobbies: if your friend plays music and you write lyrics, collaborate on a song). Play games, watch movies together using screen-sharing apps, and create your own special traditions.

 **FEELINGS MATTER**

To keep the emotional side of your friendship alive online:

○ **Send voice or video messages** to add emotions and facial expressions to your conversations.

○ **Don't hold back — express your feelings.** Instead of just nodding, say something like, "Wow, I can feel your joy!" or when you're in deep thought, share, "I need a moment to think this through." If something's funny, send a voice message with your laughter, and if you're feeling down, share that too.

○ **Use words like "hugs" and "high-five" to replace the physical touches you can't give online.**

   **MEETINGS**

Meeting up in person more often is a great idea. Physical presence strengthens the feeling of closeness. Plan activities together like a summer trip — it'll help you enrich your experience and discover sides of your friend that you can't see online.

What's next?

Take a moment to think:

- Do you have friends who make you uncomfortable or violate your personal boundaries?

- Why do you consider yourself a good friend? In what ways can you improve as a friend?

- If you don't have friends, think about the possible reasons why. How can you overcome these obstacles?

Reading material:

- "How to Know a Person: The Art of Seeing Others Deeply and Being Deeply Seen" by David Brooks

- "Never Eat Alone and Other Secrets to Success, One Relationship at a Time" by Keith Ferrazzi

- "No Is a Four-Letter Word: How I Failed Spelling but Succeeded in Life" by Chris Jericho

- "How to Win Friends and Influence People" by Dale Carnegie

Shannon Odell's TED Talk
on **"How Friendship Affects Your Brain"**

Watch and learn:

Susan Pinker's TED Talk
on **"The Secret to Living Longer May Be Your Social Life"**

Bill Bernat's TED Talk
on **"How to Connect with Depressed Friends"**

CHAPTER 5

Me and My Romantic Partners

Why Do I Need Romantic Relationships?

All your friends are diving headfirst into romantic relationships and sharing their experiences. Meanwhile, you're flying solo and wondering, "Do I need that?"

Why Are People Drawn to Romantic Relationships?

Love is one of the most profound human needs. All our relationships are driven by the desire to both give and receive love, whether it's in our relationship with ourselves or in our interactions with friends. However, romantic love holds a special place. It's the type of relationship that also involves sexual attraction (a basic need for the continuation of life). Regardless of whether or not your relationship progresses to that stage, there's an undeniable magnetic pull at its core.

When Is the Right Time?

Since romantic love is just one form of love, you might not feel the need for it right away, especially if you're feeling loved in other areas of your life. For some, this need emerges during the teenage years, while for others, it becomes more pronounced in their twenties. In any case, it's entirely up to you to decide when you're ready. Here's a simple test to help you figure it out. Which thoughts resonate with you?

So, it's perfectly normal to feel a need for romantic love and a partner, as it's biologically wired into us.

Are you waiting for love to find you, or are you being proactive?

Romantic relationships offer us:

- A stable partner to share life's adventures with.
- A shot of happiness that's like a rush of oxytocin.
- Reduced stress levels.
- Better health and a longer, more fulfilling life.

"Life is presenting so many opportunities; I'd love to share them with someone special."

"I want to be understood and accepted for who I am."

"I'd love to experience real closeness."

"I want to share my happiness."

"I'm comfortable with myself, but I'm open to exploring life with another person."

"Everyone around me is dating; maybe I should too."

"If only someone cared for me."

"There must be something wrong with me since I'm not in a relationship."

"I'm bored."

"I'm not particularly into this person, but there doesn't seem to be anyone else around."

These thoughts reflect someone who is content with themselves and ready to share their love with someone else.

On the other hand, these thoughts tend to arise when you're still working on self-acceptance.

Often, without even realizing it, we hope that romantic relationships will fill a void in our hearts because we haven't yet found love within ourselves. Or perhaps, societal norms suggest that we should have a partner during our teenage years. However, relationships built on such shaky foundations won't provide the fulfillment you seek and might bring you back to the need to start with self-love.

You should only open yourself to romantic love when you know that your happiness doesn't depend on others and that you have love to share.

Why do you need relationships?

What If I'm Afraid?

"I'm avoiding dating altogether to shield myself from potential hurt." "I'm not comfortable opening up to anyone." "I'm afraid of possibly getting hurt." Sound familiar? These fears and concerns are perfectly normal.

The start of any relationship involves a choice between safety and vulnerability. Staying within your comfort zone may feel secure, but it also means missing out on exploring the world, experiencing the wonder of closeness, and picking up invaluable communication skills.

Any attempt to open up, get close, or be vulnerable is a priceless experience. Don't expect your first romantic relationship to be perfect or last forever. Even if it's short-lived, that doesn't make it any less valuable — you're gaining experience and learning how to communicate for future, potentially long-term relationships.

How to Tell If We're a Couple

In this big world full of people, there has to be someone out there you can truly connect with. But how do you find that special someone and make the right choice? Or should you just leave it up to fate and chance?

Are You Relying on Luck or Taking Charge?

Although having a stable romantic relationship is one of the key ingredients for happiness, many of us tend to rely on fate and hope that love will magically fall into our laps. What about you? Are you waiting for love to find you, or are you out there actively searching for it?

Who Are You Looking For?

The clearer you are about the kind of person you're seeking, the easier it will be to recognize them in a crowd. To do this, start by asking yourself a few questions and analyzing your past experiences. What worked and what didn't in your previous relationships?

Being proactive means you:
- Understand who you're looking for.
- Know where to look.
- Take action.

Are you waiting for love to find you, or are you being proactive?

1 **Get to know yourself better:** your values, beliefs, lifestyle, and interests.

2 **Imagine your ideal partner,** focusing on their qualities rather than their looks. What values will they hold dear? What values do you want to share? How will they show their love for you?

4 **Where can you find this person?** Based on your interests and lifestyle, where is the best place to meet your potential partner? It could be a hiking club, a party, volunteering at an animal shelter, or even a conference about alien civilizations. (Add your ideas here.)

3 **Imagine the dynamics of your perfect relationship.** Think of it as a dance — what kind of dance will you both be doing? Will it be a waltz, salsa, or hip-hop? How often will you spend time together? Will you do things together or have deep heart-to-hearts and read books? Do you want to lead or follow? What behaviors are deal-breakers for you?

5 **Now, take action!** Now that you have a better idea of who you're looking for and where to find them, it's time to get started. Show up at places that interest you, broaden your social circle, and remember that your potential partner might be just one or two connections away, or even a friend of a friend.

Don't be afraid to initiate conversations. Every chat, even if it's brief, and every short-lived romance is a step towards finding the right person. Rejections can sting, but if you see them as part of the journey towards finding the right match, they won't seem so tough. Plus, each experience, successful or not, can help you refine your vision of your ideal partner and relationship.

So, How Do You Know If This Person Is the One?

You've met, spoke a bit, shared your first smiles, and perhaps even gone on a date or two. So, what's next? Is this person the right fit for you? The answer isn't always obvious because we're all complex individuals who can show different sides of ourselves. What separates a genuine relationship from a fleeting connection?

That magnetic attraction or strong liking.
Your initial magnetic pull toward this person doesn't fade; in fact, it might even grow stronger. You enjoy being around them, you like how they act, and you love listening to their voice. You genuinely appreciate each other and give each other heartfelt compliments. Even if you notice some flaws in their looks or behavior, they don't turn you off or make you want to run away.

Compatibility. You and your partner fit together like pieces of a puzzle. Your values, interests, habits, lifestyles, and even your friend circles align instead of clashing. Sure, there might be some differences, like one puzzle piece being more red, while the other is more blue. But these differences don't lead to cracks in your relationship; they make it deeper over time. Do you understand each other's way of thinking, support each other's passions, and share similar goals? Do you have mutual friends, and do you both enjoy hanging out with them?

Willingness to accept each other as you are. With your partner, you feel completely comfortable. You don't need to put on a mask, pretend to be someone else, or watch your words and actions. You don't have to "fix" each other or feel the urge to change each other's behavior or looks — neither yours nor your partner's. Your partner's opinions about you, your appearance, and your goals don't hurt you. You know that they fully accept you, with all your strengths and weaknesses.

Genuine communication. Besides physical attraction and the need for connection, you have meaningful conversations. As you talk, you gain a deeper understanding of each other.

Building Healthy Relationships

So, there you are, together. You're head over heels, feeling all jittery, and thinking about love. But will this feeling last forever?

Infatuation vs. Love

Infatuation and love are two different stages that often play a role in relationships. Infatuation doesn't always turn into love, and love doesn't always start with infatuation.

Infatuation is a vivid, exhilarating, but short-lived stage.

It's that intense, passionate phase where you can't get enough of each other. It's like having a major crush, and you're so into each other that you forget about everything else. During infatuation, the parts of your brain that deal with motivation and reward go into overdrive, leading to a rush of dopamine and oxytocin (the love chemicals). Psychologists say infatuation is similar to stress for your body, as it tries to find balance. This phase usually lasts for up to three months, and sometimes it ends with you waking up one day and wondering, "Who is this person, really?" If that happens, you might find yourself breaking up with the person.

Occasionally, infatuation evolves into love — that deep, steady feeling of emotional connection and fully accepting each other for who you are.

At this stage, you see each other's flaws and all that, but still adore each other. Psychologists say that love resides in a different area of the brain — the one responsible for forming bonds and connections. Building true love can take up to three years, and it involves adjusting, working through conflicts, and making discoveries.

Signs of Healthy Relationships

Healthy relationships make us better people, and they make us feel safe and confident. Here are some signs that your relationship is on the right track:

FRIENDSHIP AND FUN
You're genuine friends. You're each other's go-to person when you have news, thoughts, feelings, and ideas to share. You have loads of inside jokes. You don't take each other too seriously and playfully tease each other about your quirks or funny life moments. Playfulness, smiles, and joy are all part of your relationship.

Whether or not your infatuation turns into love depends on if you're both ready to put in the effort. It's the perfect time to share your thoughts about what makes an ideal relationship and create a shared vision for your relationship called "Us."

RESPECT
You listen to each other's opinions, ask for advice, and don't criticize or ignore each other's needs. You respect and maintain each other's boundaries.

TRUST AND HONESTY
You're honest with each other in all aspects of life. You know for sure that your partner won't hurt you, lie to you, or hide anything from you on purpose. You're open about what you expect, and you provide friendly and honest feedback. You won't shy away from telling the truth, no matter how tough it is.

KINDNESS AND EMPATHY
You treat each other with care and empathy. You listen to each other's needs and are there to support each other on tough days or provide space when necessary. In healthy relationships, both partners strive to do things that make each other happy. If someone needs help or support, you're gladly there to offer it.

SAFETY AND INDEPENDENCE
Physically and emotionally, you both feel secure. You're not afraid to be honest with each other, and you don't lay claim to each other's time or body without consent. You're free to interact with other people.

UNDERSTANDING
Do you know your partner's favorite book and why they love it? Does your partner know how long it takes you to wake up in the morning? Continuously learning new things about each other and showing interest in each other's lives is a key part of healthy relationships.

COMFORTABLE PACE
Everything in your relationship proceeds at a pace that feels comfortable for both of you. You don't feel lonely or overwhelmed by the level of interaction. This applies to everything, from the start of physical intimacy to how you spend your weekends, and how much you chat on messaging apps.

RESPONSIBILITY
In healthy relationships, both of you naturally take responsibility for the relationship and each other. This means owning up to your mistakes and apologizing when needed, being considerate of each other's thoughts and feelings, and not causing unnecessary worry. For example, if your partner goes MIA for a day, stops responding to messages, or acts distant without explanation, they're not being responsible towards the relationship or you.

YOU'RE A TEAM
You envision a future together, support each other in your individual and shared goals, and aren't afraid to have discussions. You know how to resolve conflicts and don't withdraw or get passive-aggressive when expectations aren't met. If your partner is upset, you address the issue with an open heart.

What have you achieved in your relationship so far? Which of these points might need a closer look?

How to Love and Still Be Authentic

"I feel like I've lost myself," "I'm not even sure what I want anymore," "I haven't seen my friends in 6 months." It's pretty common for romantic relationships to make you feel like you're wrapped up in your partner's world and losing sight of your own. But, could it be any other way?

Lose Yourself for a While

During the infatuation stage, it's pretty much inevitable that you'll become heavily immersed in the relationship. The crazy chemistry and biology of being in love guarantees that you're all in — it's like there's nothing and no one else in the universe except your partner. Don't try to fight it; let yourself enjoy this stage because it won't last forever. According to psychologist and relationship expert David Schnarch, losing yourself at the start of a relationship is a starting point for personal growth, both individually and as a couple. When you transition from infatuation to the stage of deep love, it's time to figure out your values, boundaries, and rules all over again. It's not just "me" anymore; it's also "we," and that changes a lot. Remember, "me" still deserves love, respect, and care. It's crucial to understand that when "me" isn't happy, "we" can't be happy either.

How to Keep Your Authenticity and Support It

TAKE GOOD CARE OF YOURSELF

Remember to take care of your body, stay active, and prioritize your health. Talk about your emotions with your partner, friends, or a psychologist. Be your own best friend, who's ready to brew you a cup of tea, sit by a pond in silence, or take a warm bath.

STAY HONEST

Honesty and open communication about your needs, feelings, and thoughts will help you stay in touch with yourself and your inner desires. Questions like what movie to watch, where to spend the weekend, or how to deal with a mutual friend should be discussed from two independently formed perspectives. Even uncomfortable topics, grudges, and suspicions should be discussed honestly. Always tell the truth gently but directly — it's a skill and a good habit.

REMEMBER YOUR VALUES AND PERSONAL GOALS

Think about and talk with your partner about what's important to you: being kind to others, respecting personal boundaries, compassion for animals, etc. This should be your list of values that you won't compromise for love and attention. It's better to create this list on paper and revisit it periodically. Your dreams and personal goals are still important. Don't give up on them just because there's an "us" now. Look for ways to balance your aspirations and help each other grow personally.

CARVE OUT SPACE AND TIME FOR YOURSELF

Spend some quality time alone — it's the most valuable time for self-reflection and connecting with your "self." Go on solo adventures — visit art galleries, museums, coffee shops, or just sit in a park with a good book. Keep up with your hobbies and personal development interests. Stay connected with your friends and occasionally enjoy some "me time." If you share a living space, designate a corner that reinforces your boundaries. Agree that you won't expect communication or contact when your partner is in that area.

Misconceptions That Can Cause You to Lose Yourself

TAKING CARE OF YOURSELF IS SELFISH

From the time we're kids, we're taught that being selfish isn't a good thing. Caring for others somehow seems like the opposite of caring for ourselves. We grow up thinking it's either you or me. So, in relationships, we're often ready to sacrifice ourselves for the sake of our loved ones. Even when our partner doesn't need that sacrifice and might not even notice it.

Constantly putting aside your own needs and wants eventually leads to deep dissatisfaction and resentment, which often ends in a breakup. But, the cycle repeats itself in new relationships because that misconception persists — if one person gains, the other must lose. **In healthy relationships, you need to learn how to find a balance that meets both people's interests and needs.**

I'M LOVED BECAUSE OF…

Another common misconception from childhood is that love has to be earned. You washed the dishes? "Good job." You got an A in school? "That's my child!" Parents, often without realizing it, tie their expressions of love to specific actions and qualities. This creates the expectation that "I'm loved for something specific, not just because." This expectation carries into romantic relationships, where our partner's love becomes tied to a particular quality (like physical appearance). If we think we're losing that quality, we fear losing love. This leads to us obsessing over maintaining that quality, turning it into the core focus. Our real needs, and often our partner's needs, get pushed aside. Can you guess how this usually ends? **True love is unconditional. A person is valued for their entirety, not just because of one specific quality.**

I'M NOTHING WITHOUT THEM

In some relationships, it feels like your entire identity revolves around being with that person. Romantic love fills the gap left by the absence of other types of love — especially self-love. You start to believe that you can only receive love in this relationship, only from this one person. This leads to dependency, unhealthy attachment, and jealousy. How long do you think such relationships can last? **The foundation of healthy relationships is realizing your inherent worth.**

Sex Is a Relationship Too

Whether you've hit that stage in your relationship or not, it's essential to remember that sex is a way for couples to connect. And the basics of healthy relationships — being honest, open, making sure both people are on the same page, and looking out for each other — become even more critical. Why?

Sex Makes You Vulnerable

Having sex means you're getting as intimately close to your partner as possible. You're sharing your thoughts, emotions, and now, your body. Usually, our body is our fortress with clear boundaries, but now, you're letting someone else in.

On top of that, we're still figuring out our sexuality, which keeps changing and growing with shared experiences. Learning about it means you've got to be open.

There's also baggage from the past, handed down from our parents and ancestors, who used to keep everything about sex a big secret. Just two generations ago, this topic was taboo and completely off-limits and never discussed within families, especially not with children. Clearly, we still carry around some of that shame and secrecy. And it's something we need to overcome to fully express our sexuality.

Despite all this, though, each generation of lovers finds the courage and love to dive into this endeavor. So, how can you make it work and keep it going?

Be True to Yourself

Listen to your instincts. Trust yourself. Love yourself. Especially now. Remember, your body is always amazing, especially when it's all about love.

Learn about yourself and explore — knowing what you genuinely want is crucial. Have an honest and open conversation with your partner about what you like, what you don't, what might hurt, or feel uncomfortable — without feeling awkward or worrying about hurting their feelings. It's your body, and it has the right to feel what it wants. Set boundaries when it comes to sex — what's acceptable, what's okay but not ideal, and what's absolutely unacceptable. For a fulfilling sex life, honesty is key.

Take Care of Each Other

Respect your partner's body and needs.

Pay attention to what your partner likes.

Never insult, make fun of, or mock your partner's body or sexual preferences.

Looking after your relationship is your responsibility too. Get checked for any sexually transmitted infections before you hot and heavy.

Trust and love mean being with only one partner until your relationship ends. This also keeps your intimate health in check.

Before engaging in sexual activity, talk about contraception. Using a condom is the safest and most straightforward method to protect your growing and developing body.

Agree on a safe word. It's a way to stop everything if one of you needs it, no matter how steamy things are getting.

Discuss how and when you'll share your preferences. Make sure the way you communicate works for both of you and doesn't mess up your vibe.

Never use force, and don't let anyone force you into anything.

If you want to try something new, ask for consent. Don't try any new moves without your partner's okay.

Don't use sex to manipulate your partner — neither by holding it back as a punishment nor giving it as a reward.

Rules for Healthy Sex

You're the only one who gets to decide when you're ready. Nobody and nothing can force you into it.

If one of you says "no," it means "no" for both of you.

No matter what kind of things you're into, none of them are bad or embarrassing if both of you are ready to explore them.

You can say "no" at any point. No stage of a relationship means you "have to" keep going.

Sex isn't a competition; there are no winners or losers, no need to be the first, most enduring, or strongest.

Experience doesn't matter; being open is everything.

Don't mix sex with alcohol. It's dangerous. Plus, your brain won't understand pleasure from sex without those substances, and you'll miss out on natural ways to feel good.

Sex needs planning — the right place and time. Planning helps avoid any awkward situations.

Sex Myths

"Guys should always make the first move." That's an old-school idea from the past when sex, especially for women, was something people felt ashamed of.

"The more partners I have, the more experienced and valuable I am." The quality and duration of relationships matter much more than the number of partners.

"Size and shape matter." Sexuality is about your brain and is influenced by lots of things. Physical attributes are only a small part of the equation.

"Everyone's having sex by age 15." The average age for people to have their first sexual experiences in most developed countries is between 16 and 18. In the United States, for example, 52% of teenagers haven't done it by age 18.

And What About "Casual Sex"?

This phenomenon can be compared to fast food — some people do it because it's convenient, some people get addicted, but very few people find true satisfaction in it. Plus, it's not great for your health. Anyway, that's not our topic. This book is about real relationships.

When Things Go Wrong

Whether it started out this way or developed over time, it doesn't matter. What matters is that you're feeling uncomfortable in your relationship. And it's pulling down your well-being. So, what kinds of relationships are we talking about here?

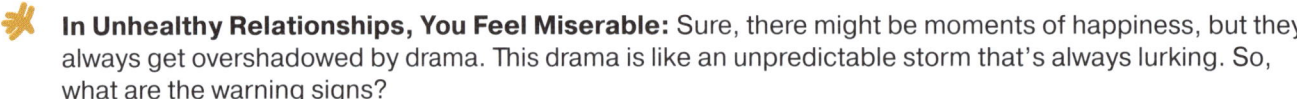

- **In Unhealthy Relationships, You Feel Miserable:** Sure, there might be moments of happiness, but they always get overshadowed by drama. This drama is like an unpredictable storm that's always lurking. So, what are the warning signs?

- **Trust Issues and Too Much Control:** "Where were you?" "Were you out playing games all night again?" "Let me see your texts." Your partner tries to control your emotions, decisions, and actions. They expect regular status updates on your whereabouts, spending, and life decisions. This constant control is a sure sign of an unhealthy relationship and a lack of trust.

- **They're Too Clingy:** You just want a quiet night in with a good book, but your partner insists on going out for a walk and gets upset when you decline. They're always around, demanding your attention 24/7. Your personal space feels like it's under siege, and you can't catch a break.

- **Manipulation:** Your partner pressures you into doing things or making decisions through guilt trips ("If you don't come with me, I'll be miserable the whole trip"), fear ("Well, I'll just find someone else then"), or obligation ("You promised you'd always be there"). Sometimes, you don't even realize you're being manipulated, but you find yourself doing things you never really wanted to do.

- **Blame Game:** You were late to the movies? Your partner had a bad day? You both forgot an important event? The blame game always points to one person — you. In unhealthy relationships, you're forced to feel guilty for everything that goes wrong.

- **All About Them:** You're not allowed to hang out with anyone else, say anything positive about anyone else, or even mention anyone else. Your partner wants to be your one and only — period.

- **Emotional Rollercoaster:** One day everything's great, but suddenly a storm hits, and you have no idea what set it off. One day your partner is showering you with attention and gifts, and the next, they're starting a fight, getting jealous, or disappearing. The longer it goes on, the wilder and scarier these emotional rollercoasters get.

- **Dishonesty:** Your partner is constantly lying to you, cheating on you, or telling you one thing while doing something else. Your partner acts differently depending on who's around — it's one way with friends, but a different way when you're alone.

- **No Respect:** Your boundaries, thoughts, feelings, hopes — none of it matters. Your partner doesn't want to hear about what's important to you, let alone consider it in your relationship. Over time, you start to believe it's your fault — that you're doing something wrong if you're being treated this way. That's not true. It's time to stand up for your self-worth.

- **Feeling Anxious:** Being with this person should feel comforting, but instead, you're always on edge, anxious, and sometimes even scared. You're scared to speak up because you don't want to trigger your partner's anger. Or you're unsure how your partner will react — by hugging you or pushing you away.

- **Physical Abuse:** No one should ever lay a hand on you. No one has the right to force you into anything you don't want to do or something that causes pain or suffering. Violence is a serious crime and goes against all the rules of healthy human relationships. There's no excuse or apology for violence. Get out of such relationships as soon as possible, and seek help if needed. And remember: it's not your fault!

How to Protect Yourself

Start a good relationship with yourself. Your self-esteem, your sense of self-worth, and knowing your value are powerful tools against these unhealthy relationships. But even if you're already in one, getting back to who you are and what's important to you is a strong first step to finding a way out.

1 From the outset, have an honest talk with your partner about what's bothering you. Use "I-messages." Sometimes, your partner might not even realize they're harming the relationship.

2 If that doesn't work, suggest taking a break to reevaluate your relationship. This break allows you to collect your thoughts, and it gives your partner a chance to think about how important the relationship is, whether they're willing to change, or if it's time to end things.

3 If problems persist after the break, firmly suggest breaking up. Don't react to threats, pleas, or attempts to make you feel sorry for them. Healthy relationships can't be built on these.

4 If you can't leave the relationship on your own, get help from a therapist or someone you trust. The key is that once you decide to break up, don't delay and don't let yourself sink deeper into the relationship. Unhealthy relationships can cause serious harm, and healing takes time.

In Addition:

Don't lose touch with your friends. Hang out with them, give them a call, and tell them how you're doing. Often, a fresh perspective from the outside helps you realize when a storm is brewing.

Trust yourself. Your inner voice usually knows what's up. If your instincts are telling you something's off, pay attention.

Keep your independence. Don't let anyone take control or limit your choices. Don't let your partner handle all the responsibilities and decisions.

Learn to say no. If something doesn't feel right, it's okay to firmly say no. Clear boundaries and the ability to stick to them are great signs of a potentially healthy relationship.

Is It Okay to Have Arguments?

We often see fights and disagreements as a bad thing, thinking that healthy relationships should always be smooth sailing. Are arguments really that dangerous? Should we try to avoid them at all costs?

Disagreements Make Your Bond Stronger

It may be hard to believe, but having arguments in a relationship doesn't always mean the end of the road for the relationship. In fact, it's normal, especially after that initial "head over heels" phase passes. Your differences don't just magically disappear, and you've got to work through them. After all, you're two separate people with different interests, opinions, and quirks. Each argument is like an opportunity to understand each other better and make your connection even stronger. The key here is to follow some smart rules for dealing with disagreements. By the way, not having any arguments at all doesn't necessarily mean everything's perfect. It could just mean you're sweeping problems under the rug.

What Doesn't Help

Some fights make things worse instead of better. Here are some signs that your arguments are more damaging than helpful:

Do you recognize any of these behaviors in yourself?

CRITICISM

Saying things like "You never clean up!", "I've asked you a million times to pick stuff up, but you never do it!", or "You're so lazy!" doesn't lead to anything good. When you criticize someone and their traits, they'll either get defensive or shut down.

CONTEMPT

Dismissive insults, sarcasm, and a rude tone just make things worse. Contempt makes it impossible to have a real conversation.

STONEWALLING

Ever seen someone act like they're a snail tucking itself away into its shell during an argument? That's stonewalling, and it's usually because the person doesn't know how to deal with conflict. They're just trying to avoid feeling hurt or scared.

BOTTLING THINGS UP

Sometimes one person just keeps letting all their annoyances pile up — dirty dishes, coming home late, not having enough fun — and then suddenly blows up with a bunch of complaints and anger, often without even knowing why they're so mad. The better way is to deal with one issue at a time, when you're just a little irritated instead of waiting until you're boiling with rage.

How to Deal with Differences in a Smart Way

To make sure that arguments help your relationship, stick to these basic rules:

STEP 1

Remember, you're a team, not enemies. When you're in a disagreement, start with the idea that you love each other and want what's best for your relationship. You're not trying to hurt each other, but something is bothering you both.

STEP 2

Explain what you're feeling and why, in as much detail as possible. Ask your partner to do the same. Use "I-statements," avoid blaming them, and don't bring up past fights. For example, say something like, "I get super worried when you disappear and don't reply to my texts. Could you please explain why you're doing this?"

STEP 3

Listen to your partner without interrupting. Don't jump to conclusions or make up stories about what they mean. Stick to the facts. So, if your partner didn't reply to a text and now says, "I was just busy," don't turn that into, "You forgot about me. You don't care."

STEP 4

Try to come up with a solution to the problem together. Your goal is to find a compromise that makes both of you happy. In a real argument, there shouldn't be a winner and loser. Instead, you can say something like, "I get it that you were busy. But I worry. What can we do so this doesn't happen again? Maybe just shoot me a quick text when you're tied up? That way, I'll know you're okay."

Extra Tips:

 **Have a "safety word" that you can say if things start to get too intense, like "timeout."** When one of you says it, take a break, calm down in separate rooms, and then come back to the conversation later.

 **Come up with a phrase one of you can use to remind the other to keep things respectful and constructive during an argument.** For example, if someone starts stonewalling, you could say, "We're adults here; we can talk things out."

 **Resolve the conflict before going to bed.** Don't let it linger, and don't hold onto grudges. It's a good habit to put arguments to rest.

 **Most importantly, remember that conflicts can only be resolved if both of you follow these rules for constructive disagreements.** You can't do it alone.

Surviving a Breakup

So, you've just gone through a breakup, which is something that happens to pretty much everyone at least once in their life. Suddenly, it's like your world has turned into a silent black-and-white movie. All those good vibes seem to have vanished, replaced by a sea of pain, hurt, and disappointment. But how can you make sure you don't completely sink into that abyss?

Breakup Causes Grief

It's crucial to understand that breaking up with someone you love is a lot like dealing with a death. It's real grief. Feeling sad, down, and even shedding a few tears is entirely normal. Don't fight these feelings, and don't be embarrassed by them. Also, don't rush the healing process, even if your friends are pushing you to "move on" and party. You need to give your feelings the time and space they deserve.

How Long Does the Hurt Last?

Imagine your situation as if you're a rocket caught in the pull of a black hole. This black hole's gravitational force is way stronger than your rocket's power, and it feels like you're losing the battle. However, your survival instincts kick in, and you start guiding your rocket away from the black hole, little by little. Eventually, you break free and get back on course. You are the pilot of that rocket. At the time of your breakup, your past relationship looks like a massive black hole, with an irresistible pull. But don't forget that survival and living life matter most. On your way to complete freedom, you'll go through several stages.

1   DENIAL
At first, you might not believe it's happening. On the one hand, this helps you shield yourself from the initial shock during those first few days. On the other hand, there's a risk that you might start ignoring reality, denying that the black hole even exists, and that could pull you in.

2   ANGER
Soon, you're flooded with anger. This anger stems from the pain and resentment you feel. You blame yourself and others for what's happened, searching for ways to release your anger and ease the pain. Anger is like a powerhouse of energy, and it's crucial to use it constructively — steer your rocket away from that black hole. Creativity and sports often help during this stage. It's no surprise that many famous songs were born out of broken hearts.

3   BARGAINING
Once your anger subsides, the pain is still there. Now, you start looking for a more rational way to deal with the situation. You explore different options, negotiate with fate, and engage in inner dialogues. Maybe there's still a chance to fix things?

4   DEPRESSION
When bargaining doesn't work, and there's no solution in sight, you fall into a state of desolation. You realize the full extent of your loss. It feels like you're inside that black hole. You're low on energy, lack the will to fight, and wake up and go to sleep thinking life is meaningless. This stage is the most dangerous and deceptive. Everything seems so dark, hopeless, and pointless. However, you're just moments away from breaking free from the black hole.

5   ACCEPTANCE
Eventually, you come to terms with your loss. You acknowledge there's no going back, but you believe it's for the best. You let go of the past for the sake of survival. You hit the "full throttle" button — heading towards open space, towards freedom, on your trajectory.

How to Help Yourself

GIVE YOURSELF TIME
Don't suppress your feelings — cry, scream, or punch a pillow if you need to. Do whatever it takes to express your pain.

BREATHE
Practice deep breathing in tough moments until the pain subsides.

SEEK OUT HELP AND TALK ABOUT IT
Surround yourself with supportive friends who understand and are willing to listen. Share your feelings and thoughts, even if they're essentially the same every day.

DREAM
Imagine how you'll feel and what you'll be doing in a year, two years, or five years. Your grief will eventually pass, and you'll gain new experiences and relationships. It's tough right now, but it won't last forever.

CUT OFF CONTACT
Stop all communication with your ex-partner. Unfollow them on social media, block their number, and archive all your shared photos. Don't let the black hole pull you back in.

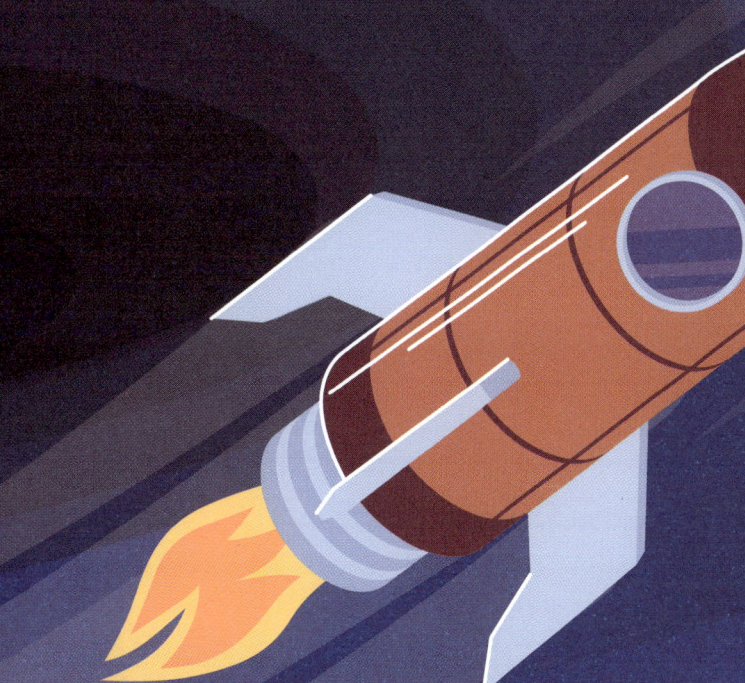

I'm the One Who Ended It…

It's rare for couples to part ways mutually. More often than not, one person takes the initiative, and it's usually tougher on the one who's left behind. If you were the one who decided to end the relationship, try to handle the breakup with care, respect, and kindness toward your past relationship.

Tell them in person. Breaking up over the phone, via text, or just ghosting someone is not a kind thing to do. The exception is if you have to escape an unhealthy relationship because of physical violence.

Explain what happened. What changed? Share your feelings honestly and openly, but kindly, without accusations.

Make it clear that it's over. Be resolute and don't give false hope.

Disappear from their life. Don't suggest just being friends; it might only prolong the pain. Accept that you're now a source of pain for your ex-partner. You'll both interpret your shared experience differently from this moment on and that's ok.

What's next?

Take a moment to think:

- How do you envision love? Think about which of these visions might have been influenced by your parents' relationships.

- Describe your ideal partner with 10 traits. Then, reread them and cross out 5 that are not essential to you or are influenced by societal expectations.

- Do you change your habits, interests, and values when you start dating someone? Make a list of your values and principles that you promise not to compromise on for any relationship.

Reading material:

- "Conscious Loving: The Journey to Co-Commitment" by Gay Hendricks and Kathlyn Hendricks

- "Getting the Love You Want: A Guide for Couples" by Harville Hendrix

- "Eat, Pray, Love" by Elizabeth Gilbert

- "The 5 Love Languages: The Secret to Love that Lasts" by Gary Chapman

Watch and learn:

Katie Hood's TED Talk
on **"The Difference Between
Healthy and Unhealthy Love"**

Helen Fisher's TED Talk
on **"Why We Love, Why We
Cheat"**

CHAPTER 6
Me and
My Crew

Me and My Crew

Humans are naturally social creatures. We're stronger together than when we are alone. Even if you're not the social butterfly type, there are times when you'll need some social interaction, help, and support, preferably from your crew. So, what exactly is your circle, and how do you find it?

Spotting the Difference Between Friends and Strangers

Throughout life, we enter various social groups — from small cliques to large communities — based on where we're born, where we go to school, or where we work. We're born into a social group automatically: our family. As we grow up, we become part of a school class or join groups based on shared interests. But not all the groups we end up in are our crew. From the day we feel we need like-minded folks, we have the freedom to search for and choose them. So, who are they?

- **Some people just click with us right away** — even if we've known them for just a day. Hanging out with them feels easy and comfortable. They accept us for who we are, help us unleash our potential, overcome life's obstacles, and reach new heights. And, of course, we're ready to do the same for them. These are the people who make up our crew.
- **At the same time, there are others** with whom we might feel out of place or misunderstood. Every word we say seems out of sync, and they simply don't get our jokes. It might even make us feel scared or embarrassed to be ourselves. That's a clear sign that we're among strangers.

Having shared values, empathy, and support forms the bedrock of a tight-knit group. If you constantly feel on edge, awkward, or give up on your beliefs to fit in, chances are that the group isn't a great fit.

Now, you've got some options:

YOU CAN STICK AROUND AND CHANGE YOURSELF TO BLEND IN WITH THE GROUP. This is often the route taken by people with weak self-identity and low self-esteem who are heavily influenced by what others think.

YOU CAN RESHAPE THE GROUP TO ALIGN BETTER WITH YOUR VALUES AND BELIEFS. Leaders often do this when they see the potential in the group and believe in it.

YOU CAN LEAVE AND CONTINUE SEARCHING FOR YOUR TYPE OF PEOPLE. This is a move made by someone mature, who understands their core values. Ultimately, you don't need the entire world to accept you; you need to live with people who embrace your true self.

Finding Your Crew

While there's no universal formula for finding like-minded people, here are some tips:

TAKE A GOOD LOOK AT YOURSELF.
Reflect on your values. What's non-negotiable for you? What do you value in people? In yourself? What's your group meant to provide?

LOOK AROUND. There might be people close by who share many of your interests; you just haven't had a chance to connect with them yet.

MAKE THE FIRST MOVE. Lots of people shy away from making new acquaintances. But reaching out can help bridge the gap and build closer relationships, even if you risk being told no.

BE YOURSELF. While it's tempting to change yourself to fit into a "cool" group, being genuine and open is the best way to find your crew.

BE AWARE OF YOUR INTERESTS.
How do you like spending your time? Maybe you can't imagine life without video games or you're all about skateboarding until the wee hours. It's often easier to find your crew among those who share your interests.

STEP OUT INTO THE WORLD.
Meeting new people isn't likely to happen while you're cooped up indoors. Attend the first volleyball practice, volunteer at an animal shelter, or sign up for Spanish classes. Taking action is key.

DON'T RUSH IT. Feeling a bit awkward in a new group is completely normal. Give others a chance to get to know you better, and take a good look at the people around you too.

What to Do If You're Surrounded by Strangers

Often, we find ourselves on the outside just because we're different from the rest. Just like the main character in "The Ugly Duckling." But being different doesn't mean something is wrong with you.

Remember, your current surroundings aren't the whole world. Your flock of beautiful white swans is out there somewhere; you just have to keep searching. Join clubs related to your interests, travel, engage in discussions, and participate in activities you're passionate about. At the very least, you'll broaden your horizons, and at best, you'll find your like-minded crew.

The more naturally and honestly you carry yourself, the higher the chances of attracting people who share your values. And remember, they're looking for you too!

The Life Cycles of a Group

Just like any living creature, a group is always changing and evolving. Some people join it, others leave, and some come back. How does a group grow? How can you handle the ups and downs of the first days in a new crew? And how do you know when it's time to move on?

How a Group Lives

Although each group is unique and has its own vibe — whether it's a sports team or a book club — they all follow the same path of development.

A psychologist named Bruce Tuckman broke down a group's journey into five stages:

1. **FORMING:** People start getting to know each other, as they play it safe, test the waters, and try out different roles. The key at this stage is communication, so don't hesitate to talk to others and ask questions.

2. **STORMING:** This is when everyone figures out how they all fit together. Conflicts arise, positions are contested, and everyone's got their own opinions. If you're eyeing a leadership role, this is your time to shine.

3. **NORMING:** The group starts forming close bonds. They realize they're a team and they believe in each other, as they develop a sense of unity. The group members start tackling tasks together, not on their own. Don't forget to acknowledge each member's contribution here.

4. **PERFORMING:** The Golden Period — those who make it to this stage (which is only around 17% of groups) can be called a dream team. Things run smoothly — everyone knows each other's worth and they're all in it for the common good.

5. **ADJOURNING:** The group comes to an end. This typically happens when they've achieved all their goals, like when a summer camp wraps up or a project is completed. Sometimes, people just get interested in something else. Feeling a bit down or worried during this phase is normal.

Understanding the stages a group goes through can help you better understand the difficulties that arise and help your team work through them.

How to Behave in a New Group

Fitting into a new group can be tricky, especially if everyone else has known each other for a while. In those early days, it might feel like others are watching your every move and sizing you up. The idea of being a newcomer can be intimidating, and the fear of not being accepted is natural. Everyone in the group feels this during the forming stage. Here are some tips to help you settle in quickly:

- **Observe those around you.** How do they act, and what are they interested in? Communication will flow easier if you find common ground.

- **Introduce yourself.** Don't wait for the group to notice you. Just say hello and ask a question; that's a good way to start.

- **Keep it friendly.** People enjoy being around someone who smiles and listens.

- **Be yourself.** Trying too hard to please everyone can come off as fake. Plus, you'll only find like-minded people if you stay true to yourself.

- **Avoid criticism.** Starting a conversation with criticism isn't a great idea. It's better to try to understand where the other person's coming from and why they think or act that way.

- **Take the lead.** Suggest going out for coffee or taking a walk during a break. If your idea doesn't catch on, don't be discouraged; people are still getting to know you.

- **Ask questions.** Find out where the cafeteria is or where is the best place to have lunch. People feel important and close when they lend a hand.

How to Know When It's Time to Say Goodbye

Not every group is meant to be lifelong friends, and that's okay. Sometimes, relationships run their course and become as worn out as an old pair of sneakers. Knowing when to say goodbye is important. It's the only way to move forward and find a new group for the next chapter of your life.

Think about whether it's time to move on if:

Your values start to clash. Maybe you used to love partying together, but now you're focused on your studies. People change over time, and it's perfectly normal for those changes to affect your relationships and group involvement.

You're constantly hiding something because you're afraid of judgment — like a new hobby, job, or friendship. It means trust between you and the group is fading, and you don't feel safe anymore.

Socializing wears you out instead of energizing you. Instead of feeling recharged, you feel drained after hangouts. So, you start making excuses to skip the next get-together.

You're only bonded by memories. When you meet up, you spend more time reminiscing than talking about what's happening in your lives right now. Nostalgia is fine, but it shouldn't be the main thing holding your relationships together.

Opening up has become tough. You're no longer interested in sharing news from your life or expressing your opinions and thoughts.

Ending on the Right Note

Have an honest conversation about how your interests are changing and how you're moving on to the next stage in your life. Show gratitude for what the group has given you. If close bonds have faded away, you can slowly reduce contact, and your interactions will naturally decrease. Don't just ghost or block the group on social media. Remember, the plume of our interactions with people follows us for life. What kind of plume it is depends on your maturity and wisdom in handling relationships.

Your Place in the Group

Finding your crew is just the beginning. It's just as important to figure out your place within it. How can you tell which role suits you best? And can a single person handle more than one role in a group?

The Need for Roles in a Group

In any group, everyone gets assigned roles based on their skills, needs, and personality. These roles help keep the group stable and make it easier for everyone to succeed together. You can't perform all roles at once or be good at all of them. The best results come from having each other's backs.

To understand the importance of roles in a group, picture an orchestra. If you hand a violin bow to the drummer, put the pianist behind a double bass, and take the conductor's baton away, you'll end up with chaotic noise instead of a pleasant melody. But when each member is in their proper place, the orchestra plays smoothly.

Different Types of Roles

Think about when you watch a movie; you can instantly recognize certain characters — one who cracks jokes to lighten the mood, or another who plans out everything meticulously. These are roles in action, and they exist in real life too.

TEAM-WORKER

Always listens, helps, and supports. When a fight's about to break out, they're the first to say, "Let's not argue!" and they'll do whatever it takes to get the group back on track.

PLANT

Always coming up with fresh ideas. They think outside the box, even though they might miss some details.

SPECIALIST

Possesses the skills and knowledge required for a specific task. They're the ones who know exactly what to do.

Psychologist Meredith Belbin identified nine types of group roles. They might not sound the same in real life, but they're still there:

SHAPER

The one who pushes the group forward. They seemingly don't care about the challenges; they see them as opportunities. Even when things get tough, shapers stay positive and hype up their crew.

COORDINATOR

Can spot everyone's strengths and knows how to use them. Like a ship captain, they steer the team towards its goal.

RESOURCE INVESTIGATOR

Extremely curious and sociable. They're always interested in what's happening with others and what opportunities are out there, and they love sharing their findings with the group.

COMPLETER FINISHER

Thinks through ideas proposed by others. They weigh the pros and cons and sometimes offer criticism.

IMPLEMENTER

Turns ideas into action. They're the driving force you can rely on to get stuff done.

MONITOR EVALUATOR

Spots mistakes and errors. They remind the group about deadlines and pay attention to details.

One person can take on multiple roles. For example, you might be both a plant and a team-worker. In some cases, your role might change entirely — like if you're the only one who knows how to set up a tent on a camping trip!

Which Role Is the Most Important?

We often think the role of the leader — that charismatic, inspiring figure who guides the group — is the most important. However, in a group full of leaders, there's no one to turn those bold ideas into reality. Without the "worker bees" and the good organizers, ideas will stay just that — ideas. The key to a successful group is to find a balance in people's roles and abilities, while respecting each person's contribution. In a successful team, people complement each other and share responsibilities. Teams with only one type of role are only good for specific tasks, like brainstorming for a creative project. But for long-term collaboration, diversity is key.

Can Roles Change?

Absolutely! Your personality and character can influence your role in a group. You might naturally be punctual and quickly earn the label of "the timekeeper." But remember, you're more than just a label like an "extrovert" or "introvert." Throughout life, we change and grow. Your role should allow for personal development and not hold you back. Don't be afraid to try out different roles, and don't sweat the mistakes — they're just part of your journey toward self-realization.

Which role do you think fits you? And which one feels like a mismatch?

Should Anyone Strive to Be a Leader?

Everyone has tried being a leader at least once. It's the most significant but also the most responsible role. It inspires some people and scares others. How do you know if it's for you?

Who Is a Leader?

Is it the person at the top? Whose opinion is the law? Who dominates and gets others to do things? All of these ideas are like remnants from way back when. A modern leader is quite different from that all-powerful image.

A true leader is someone who can influence and inspire people to work together towards a goal. Contemporary leaders make a group better by helping each member become the best version of themselves.

And you don't need to sit on a throne or have people under your command. It can be a blogger, a teacher, or a doctor — these are examples of what we call modern leadership. The job you choose doesn't limit you; it's all about how much you're into leading and growing.

Leaders Aren't Born, They're Made

There's a misconception that leadership is a talent that only a few are born with. However, many life stories prove the opposite: everyone has leadership qualities. Whether it shows up in you depends on your choices and willingness to grow. The closest area where you can practice leadership is your own life. Get inspired, create a vision for the future, set goals, take action, and take responsibility for yourself. As the leader of your own life, you're the captain of your ship, steering your course, not just a passenger on the ship at the mercy of external forces.

To Be a Good Leader, You Must First Be a Good Person

Someone who understands and shows empathy to others. Strength comes from accepting weaknesses. Being generous and compassionate. Recognizing the best parts of human nature and helping others bring those out.

Robin Sharma, a Canadian writer and leadership expert, believes that a true leader follows these principles:

 **A leader doesn't need a title or status.** Anyone can influence people regardless of their formal role in a social group.

 Leadership is built on positive relationships with people. Your actions should benefit both the group and you. You should genuinely understand your colleagues, group members, and clients. Care about those you interact with, and don't forget to add some fun, joy, and real enjoyment to what you do.

 **Great leaders emerge from great people:** those who work tirelessly on themselves, push their limits, learn, grow spiritually and mentally, develop physically, and can control their mood and mindset.

 **Leaders emerge in all kinds of times.** Tough situations can bring out the brightest leaders. Don't be scared of change — it's the perfect time to awaken the leader in you and motivate people to move towards the future.

To Lead, You Need Special Qualities

Tony Robbins, a motivational speaker and leadership expert, identifies 13 key qualities of a true leader:

1. Confidence.
2. Focus on the essentials.
3. A vision for the future.
4. The ability to inspire.
5. Resilience in the face of stress, setbacks, and difficulties.
6. Honesty with oneself and others.
7. Positive attitude and optimism.
8. Determination.
9. Effective communication.
10. Taking responsibility for both successes and failures.
11. Empathy.
12. Humility.
13. Creativity.

Which of these qualities do you already possess? And which ones have surprised you the most?

Is This for Me?

One of the great things about being human is to possess free will. There's a choice in every situation. Whether you want to be a leader or not is up to you. Make your decision based on what feels right for you, not what others expect. If you want to be the leader of your own life — that's great. If you prefer a professional path in a specialized field with minimal interaction — that's also fine. Just don't make this choice out of fear. Try things out before you decide.

I'm Not Sure I Wanna Do It

Relationships within a group aren't always smooth sailing and harmonious. Sometimes, there's conflict between you and those around you. So, what do you do when the group tries to push a certain behavior on you? And how do you handle it when things start to get ugly?

Dealing with Group Pressure

Chances are, you've come across group pressure at some point — maybe from friends, classmates, or coworkers. It usually happens when there's a clash between one person's interests and what the group is seeking. The idea behind group pressure is to get us to do things we wouldn't normally do. Like skipping class or messing with someone's stuff.

In the mid-20th century, American psychologist Solomon Asch showed just how much influence a group can have on an individual. With a series of experiments, he demonstrated that two-thirds of all participants change their opinions under pressure from a group even if they were right initially.

Group pressure isn't always obvious. Sometimes, those around you don't have to try hard to influence your behavior — you just follow their lead. They might wear certain clothing or listen to a particular artist, and you might find yourself doing the same. But often, pressure can be more obvious and manipulative. It could involve compliments, flattery, excessive attention, persuasion, and sometimes even teasing, threats, or blackmail.

We often give in to group pressure because we're afraid of being isolated from the crowd. Going against the group means stepping into the unknown and taking charge of our lives. But that's precisely what mature individuals do. They make decisions independently, guided by their inner values, rather than following the crowd.

What to Do When the Group Pressures You

Just say no. You don't have to get into a debate.

Decline and offer an alternative. For instance, if you can't go to the movies today, suggest going on Saturday.

Be honest about your reasons for saying no. Feeling tired or having other plans for the day is a valid excuse.

Buy yourself some time. Promise to think about the proposal and come back with an answer when you're sure about your choice.

Find someone who's on the same page as you. It's easier to stand up for yourself when you have a partner.

If the situation escalates and becomes uncomfortable, remember — you always have the right to walk away.

Understanding Bullying and How to Deal with It

Bullying is a kind of persistent aggression aimed at some person. If you're constantly being insulted, teased, excluded, pushed around, beat up, cornered on your way home, intimidated, mocked, or having your money taken, you're dealing with bullying.

Bullying often starts as a joke. But the key difference between bullying and harmless humor is that the abuse doesn't stop; instead, it becomes progressively more cruel and degrading.

You might think there must be a specific reason you're being bullied. You might even say, "Well, maybe it's my fault." That's not true! Anyone can become a target: the quiet high-achiever, someone from a different background, or the new kid in class. It's not about "who" the victim is; it's about the group developing such behavior. They're breaking the norm. There are no justifications or valid reasons for cruelty.

Who Is Affected by Bullying?

Bullying hurts everyone, including bystanders. When we witness insults and mockery, we no longer feel safe. If they bully one person today, they might target someone else tomorrow. This traps us in a fear-based dilemma: we know what's happening is wrong, but we're too scared of becoming the next victim, and we might even side with the aggressor. This is why many observers either join the bully or turn a blind eye to the bullying. Later in life, they deeply regret this.

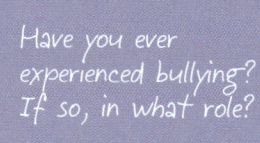

Have you ever experienced bullying? If so, in what role?

ahahah

How to Handle Bullying

It's tough to combat bullying. It makes you feel alone and helpless, and sometimes it seems like there's no way out. When it comes to bullying, the saying "strength in numbers" holds true. You can get support from your friends. Or it might be best to seek help from a trusted adult.

Here are a few tips that might help you handle bullying:

- **Keep believing in your self-worth.** You're awesome just as you are!
- **Remember, what others say about you doesn't define your reality.** Being called names doesn't make you any less valued.
- **Try to stay calm.** Reacting emotionally is like fuel for the bully's fire.
- **Initially, you might try talking to the bully.** What's causing their behavior? Sometimes, there's a misunderstanding, and the conflict can be resolved. But don't do it if things have gone too far and scare you.
- **Take action to protect yourself.** Don't fall for intimidation tactics. When someone says, "If you tell anyone, it'll get worse," they're just afraid of facing the consequences of their actions.

My Friends Have a Cooler Life Than Me

One of your friends went to see a super popular show, another went to the beach, and the third managed to squeeze in a five-mile run bright and early. Meanwhile, your life feels kind of dull, uninspiring, and repetitive. Sound familiar? Well, maybe you've got a case of FOMO.

What's FOMO, You Ask?

FOMO stands for Fear of Missing Out. It's that nagging worry that everyone else is doing something cool, important, and interesting while you're stuck in a slump.

FOMO stems from the need to feel like a part of a group, have a certain status within it, and constantly connect with others. When you feel like you're missing out, your brain's alarm bells start ringing. Next thing you know, you're getting ready for a late-night museum visit when your original Friday night plan was to crash early.

Here are some signs of FOMO:

You constantly refresh your social media, and you get seriously upset when you can't get online.

You try to be everywhere at once. Sleep, relaxation, and your passions all take a backseat.

You feel down because you're comparing your life to others.

But why do you feel like everyone else is living it up, while you're just stuck in a rut?

The fear of missing out on fun events or great opportunities has been around for ages, but social media has dialed it up a notch. Now, we're constantly peeking into other people's lives, which makes it easy to compare ourselves to them.

There's usually an underlying cause behind a strong FOMO. It might be a sign that:

 You are lonely and feel disconnected from people.

 You are unhappy with your life. When we're not content, we tend to worry more about what others are doing.

Take a moment to think about why you feel like everyone else is living it up, and why what you're doing right now doesn't seem to be enough.

You feel like an outsider if you can't be at an event or hang out with friends.

You can't commit to one thing — you keep trying new hobbies, but you never really dive into one particular thing.

You have low self-esteem, want to show off to others, and feel like you have to keep tabs on your "competition".

You are facing a super tough and important decision.

How Can You Tackle That Fear of Missing Out?

Start by figuring out what you want. Sure, you could rush off to catch the last day of that art exhibition, then pop by a ceramics workshop, and finish the day with a new coding course. But before you do all that, ask yourself: why do I want to do all this stuff?

Set priorities. Maybe you've been pouring all your energy into school for a whole year, and now you want to hang out more with your friends. In that case, will a new intensive foreign language class make you happier?

Limit your social media time. Try turning off those extra notifications and setting some boundaries for your apps. If someone's posts bug you or bring you down, hide them from your feed and keep the ones that inspire you. And think about it, do you need to check social media every day? Maybe once a week is plenty.

Learn to appreciate boredom. Being bored can actually be really productive. It lets your mind wander and sparks your imagination.

Lastly, appreciate what you have. Learn to enjoy what you're doing right here and now. Even if it's just chilling in bed with a book on the weekend. There will always be something better out there, but will chasing after it make your life fuller and you happier?

Remember, social media is just a highlight reel of people's lives — usually the best parts, and sometimes, it's a bit exaggerated. Your friend probably won't share their latest flop, but they'll happily post photos from a concert by their favorite band.

What's next?

Take a moment to think:

- How does the group you're part of influence your values? Do you like this influence?

- Does your environment inspire self-improvement and motivate you to be the best version of yourself? Why or why not?

- List 5 traits of the crew or group you'd like to be a part of. Where can you find such a group?

Reading material:

- "The Charisma Myth: How to Engage, Influence and Motivate People" by Olivia Fox Cabane

- "Attached: The New Science of Adult Attachment and How It Can Help You Find — and Keep — Love" by Amir Levine and Rachel Heller

- "Outliers: The Story of Success" by Malcolm Gladwell

- "Connected: The Surprising Power of Our Social Networks and How They Shape Our Lives" by Nicholas Christakis and James Fowler

Nicholas Christakis's TED Talk on **"The Hidden Influence of Social Networks"**

Watch and learn:

Roselinde Torres's TED Talk on **"What It Takes to Be a Great Leader"**

Kio Stark's TED Talk on **"Why You Should Talk to Strangers"**

Me and the World

My World Is a Reflection of Me

The people around you and your relationships with them. The stories and the meaning you attach to them. Your room, your city, your country, and finally, our planet. It's all your world, and how you see it is up to you. It's like a mirror that you look into every single day.

So, What's Your World Like?

Your world isn't some fierce beast waiting for you to make a mistake. It's neither bad nor good, neither loving nor rejecting. It's just a collection of events and circumstances. Your perspective and expectations paint your world with different colors, giving meaning to various events. Looking at the world through a yellow-tinted lens might bring you joy; if it's a dark green lens, it might make you cautious and nervous, but if it's clear and transparent, you're probably closer to reality!

I Am the World

Your perceptions and mindset are the key to how you experience the world. Here are just a few of them:

SELF-ESTEEM

The less you value yourself, the less significant you feel, even among your closest circle. Thoughts like "Nobody cares about me," "They think I'm stupid," and "I'm the worst" make us see the world as an unfriendly, unpleasant place.

BELIEFS AND CONVICTIONS

"Girls should be obedient," "If I cry, no one will want to talk to me," "If you're different from everyone else, there's something's wrong with you." These beliefs that society feeds you can make you feel out of touch with reality and uncomfortable when you don't fit the mold.

COGNITIVE BIASES

Sometimes, we get stuck thinking one way or relying on stereotypes, which traps us. For instance, if we have an argument with someone in the morning, we might not notice any of the good things that happen throughout the day. We don't listen to the other side in a fight; we just label it as nonsense. When we let our brains run on autopilot and stick to our well-worn thought paths, we miss seeing the bigger picture and understanding our place in the world.

MEMORY OF PAST EXPERIENCES

Adverse events from the past often stick with us and can limit our perception of reality. For instance, you wanted to join a group, but they rejected you. Since then, you've thought deep friendships just don't exist. Is that true? Not even close. But we keep feeling like it is because our brain's limbic system wants to protect us from imagined threats. That's why it's good to engage the frontal lobes that help you analyze, recognize, and accept reality.

Cognitive biases, beliefs, and limits are signs that our thinking has become rigid. If you're uncomfortable, scared, or life feels heavy in your world, it's essential to work on being more flexible and aware of your thoughts.

Changing Your Perspective on the World

Sometimes, stereotypes and beliefs help us save time by assigning labels to familiar things, avoiding the need to spend too much energy thinking about them. However, these same labels can stop us from changing and keep our thinking in a box.

That's why it's essential to develop a growth mindset. Psychologist Carol Dweck coined this term. It means staying open-minded, curious, and interested in new things, different points of view, and unfamiliar things.

Flexibility and staying open-minded also helps you to keep up with the world. Your surroundings, people, and you yourself are constantly changing, plus new technologies keep popping up that can make life more complicated. A growth mindset helps us adapt to changes.

- **Fixed mindset:** I've got this whole world figured out. Anything that doesn't match what I know is either a lie or an enemy.
- **Growth mindset:** You can't know everything about the world; one life isn't enough. Every opinion and thing has a right to exist, and they don't need my approval.

From Fixed to Growth Mindset

The core of flexible thinking is mindfulness, or seeing things from an observer's perspective. The less we get stuck in our experiences and beliefs, the more we become observers (not critics) of what's happening, and the more interesting and exciting our world becomes.

Listen to your thoughts. If you're making generalizations, applying labels, or using clichés, notice it and shift your focus to reality.

Feel your thoughts and emotions. Ask yourself questions like: "What do I believe? What triggered this thought or emotion?"

Embrace the new. Don't reject strange ideas and people or new and unfamiliar things. Learn more; don't rush to form an opinion.

Use positive beliefs. Instead of saying, "I can't do anything right," tell yourself, "I can do it all, and I'm worthy of love anyway."

What's Going On in the World

We often hear pretty worrisome news about military conflicts, the spread of diseases and much more. It feels like the world is going down the tubes. But is that true?

What Is the Modern World Like?

All countries are moving forward, although at different speeds. If you look at some key facts, you can see that today's world is much better than it was 50 years ago. People are living longer, and fewer children are dying young. There are fewer wars and less violence overall, and we're getting closer to defeating hunger and reducing social inequality. According to historian Yuval Harari, humanity has finally started embracing empathy and compassion, and now these values extend to all humans and animals. People generally take responsibility for the world around them and are ready to work together and find compromises for the greater good. Throughout all of history, today is the best time to be alive, even if it might not seem that way in specific places or situations.

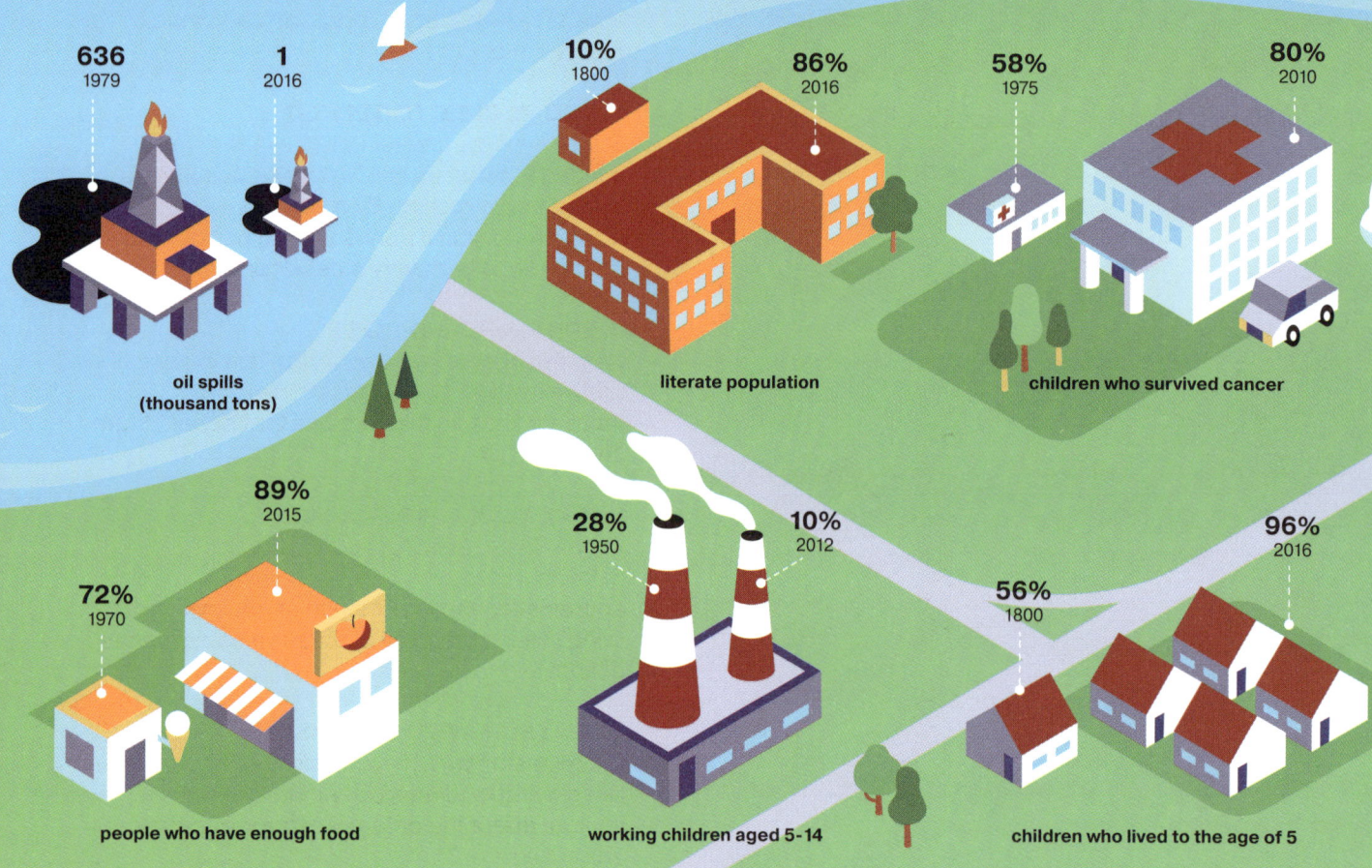

636 1979   **1** 2016
oil spills (thousand tons)

10% 1800   **86%** 2016
literate population

58% 1975   **80%** 2010
children who survived cancer

72% 1970   **89%** 2015
people who have enough food

28% 1950   **10%** 2012
working children aged 5-14

56% 1800   **96%** 2016
children who lived to the age of 5

But Why Does It Seem Like Something's Not Right with the World?

It's because of perspective — the way we look at things. It's tough to see the big picture and long-term trends when you just live your daily life. But if you step back and compare life today to how it was a century ago, you'll see progress, and not just in the more developed countries.

In your opinion, where is the world at right now in terms of progress?

So, Where Does Your World Currently Stand in its Development?

Every person deserves happiness, respect, and a life free from suffering, which is the main idea of humanism — the overall concept behind the current development stage of the world.

Each person is like a piece of a much larger puzzle called humanity. And just like any puzzle piece, you can influence the people and things around you, which then has a ripple effect on the rest of the world. Each of us has a role in living peacefully and lovingly with ourselves and others.

What are you already doing from this list? What can you add to your life?

What Can You Do to Make Your World Better?

We shape the world through interactions with the people close to us: our friends, family, and partners. And they, in turn, influence their circles, creating a chain reaction that eventually shapes the entire world. So, if you want to change something or simply spread love in the world, take action.

REGULARLY ASK YOURSELF, "WHAT DO I WANT TO SHARE WITH THE WORLD?"

This vital question will help you find meaning in your daily activities and interactions. Life isn't about what you get but what you give. What can you do to help others? What positive things can you bring to the world? Whether going for a walk, working, or reading, you can make a positive impact.

BRING PEOPLE TOGETHER

Start meetups, create communities of like-minded individuals, and take part in activities that promote growth. By doing this, you'll build strong social bonds among people and contribute to humanity's development.

INSPIRE AND SUPPORT

Help the people you care about feel valued and less alone. Support their ideas and motivate them to take actions that benefit them and the world.

SHARE YOUR KNOWLEDGE

Do you have skills like taking care of animals, respecting personal boundaries, or appreciating the importance of minimalistic living? Help spread all of these valuable pieces of knowledge!

EMPATHIZE WITH OTHERS

Practice empathy. If you want to do something, like playing loud music at night, think about how it might affect the different groups of people around you.

SHARE YOUR IDEAS AND VISION

If you dream of having a cleaner neighborhood, suggest a community cleanup with your neighbors. If you see the world as an inclusive place, talk with your school about setting up a cultural club for any nation, race, or gender to discuss your differences and similarities.

What Problems Can I Solve?

Even though the world is moving forward and improving in many ways, there are still some big problems, and new challenges keep emerging. But you and I can make a difference in solving them, and that's not an exaggeration!

Global Challenges

Even though we've made progress in reducing hunger and poverty, there are some serious global problems that we need to tackle. Yuval Harari talks about three significant challenges we're facing today:

Preventing nuclear war. Nuclear weapons could wipe out the entire world, causing chaos and death. Our job is to do everything possible to ensure that countries prioritize agreements over weapons.

Dealing with the scary consequences of global warming. We need to switch entirely to green energy sources, drastically reduce carbon emissions, and learn to live in harmony with nature if we want a future for our children and grandchildren on this planet.

Figuring out how to use advanced technologies without losing our jobs. Artificial intelligence is getting so clever that it might replace many jobs, which could result in lots of people being unemployed. We need to find a way for tech to help us, not hurt us.

These challenges might seem vast and impossible to tackle without help. However, we can all contribute at our own level. For example, recycling may be a solution to a global problem that happens locally. Recognizing the issue and taking action within your reach is something anyone can do.

How Can I Tackle Big Problems?

Imagine if every person on Earth spent just an hour planting a single tree. By evening, our whole planet would be covered in new saplings. Your contribution might seem small right now, but the more people chip in, even in tiny ways, the faster we can deal with global problems.

1

BE A LIVING EXAMPLE OF LOVE FOR YOURSELF, your loved ones, your city, your country, humanity, nature, and the world. Think of every action you take as an expression of love, not hate.

2

TAKE RESPONSIBILITY. It's easy to say, "It's not my problem," and dodge responsibility. But here's the thing: what happens in your family, your company, your street, your country, and the world affects you directly! Your present and future depend on these events and your reactions to them.

DEVELOP YOUR CRITICAL THINKING SKILLS. Learn to tell fact from fiction, cause from effect, and what matters from what doesn't. Use multiple sources of information. Without this skill, you'll get lost in the endless info stream and fall for manipulation and propaganda. Thinking for yourself is a crucial trait for a modern person.

3

4

VISUALIZE THE FUTURE. Keep an image of the kind of world you want to live in. Do you want to be surrounded by people who treat each other with respect and care? Do you want a clean and cozy environment? Align your actions with your vision of the future.

Start with Yourself

You are an essential part of humanity. What you do directly impacts the people around you and the world as a whole. So, start with yourself.

What small action can you take today?

Small Actions, Big Impact

You can solve big problems by doing small things. Building a massive, sturdy house isn't a one-person job, but when everyone pitches in, it gets done. Small actions represent your contribution to a bigger shared future:

BE AN ACTIVE CITIZEN. Join discussions about improving your local area, suggest ideas for renovating parks, participate in elections, and don't stay silent in the face of injustice — speak up. The way your city, country, and the world look is your business.

VOLUNTEER. Choose a cause you feel strongly about, whether helping homeless people, people with disabilities, caring for abandoned animals, or planting trees.

BE MINDFUL OF YOUR IMPACT ON THE ENVIRONMENT. Conserve water and electricity, avoid buying stuff you don't need, no more single-use plastics, and don't litter. Encourage these practices within your circle.

RESPECT YOUR SURROUNDINGS. According to the Broken Windows Theory, if one window in a house is broken and left unfixed, all the windows will soon be broken. The idea is that the condition of your environment directly affects the crime level and well-being of your city and its residents.

CHOOSE RESPECT AND EMPATHY OVER AGGRESSION. Anger, hatred, and the urge to be rude are wild, knee-jerk reactions. Expressing them won't help you or the world progress. Always go for respect and compassion as higher-level responses that modern, cultured people should aim for. Help those in need, spread smiles and good vibes, and watch the positivity spread.

Nature Deserves Love Too

Urbanization and the growth of consumerism used to be seen as signs of progress. However, we're starting to see the consequences of our never-ending desire for more. We've lost our connection with nature and jeopardized the planet and ourselves. Is there a way out of this mess?

The Consequences of Lost Touch

The industrial age and thoughtless exploitation of natural resources have put humanity on the brink. Most scientists agree that, with the current levels of greenhouse gas emissions, living on this planet will be a real challenge this century. Here are just a few numbers to paint the picture:

- Half a billion people will suffer from a lack of drinking water every day.

- Almost half of all tropical forests are going to disappear.

- Global temperatures and sea levels are rising, meaning coastal areas and fertile farmland will be underwater.

- Crop yields will drop by 10-15%, leading to hunger.

- People will have to deal with extreme weather, like unbearable heat and cold, droughts, and floods.

Reconnecting with Nature

We care for the things we love, and we love the things we know. Now is the time to learn and reconnect with nature.

SPEND MORE TIME OUTDOORS. Instead of reading at home, head to the park with a blanket. Swap that café meetup with friends for a walk in the woods. Collect leaves for a nature scrapbook, plant some flowers and trees, and learn to care for living beings. The more time you spend in nature, the closer your connection will become and the more love you'll feel.

PAY ATTENTION. Be mindful in your approach to the time you spend outside. Even just walking to the store, there's so much to notice: the sunlight filtering through leaves, birds caring for their young, or the bark of trees nibbled by insects. Quiet your thoughts and observe — it helps to see the nature around you, feel connected, and regain your inner balance.

LEARN. To truly appreciate nature, you need to learn more about it. Find a topic that interests you. It could be ecology or birds. Or maybe you've always been curious about where those May beetles come from. Look for information, read up, and observe these intriguing phenomena.

What's a natural event that made you stop and take notice recently?

Is the situation really that dire? Unfortunately, yes. Our planet is hurting because of what we humans are doing to it. Our job is to nurse it back to health and ensure our future generations have a place to live. Every little action counts in this fight. As writer Jonathan Safran Foer said, "Our ability to undo the damage we've done depends on collective acts of will."

What Can You Do to Save the Planet?

The most important thing anyone can do is reduce their carbon footprint in their daily life.

WALK or use a bike, scooter, or skateboard to get around the city.

ONLY BUY WHAT YOU CAN EAT. Go for seasonal, locally-grown produce to shrink the carbon footprint of your groceries.

MINIMIZE WASTE. Make it a habit to bring reusable bags when shopping and avoid plastic containers and bags.

SORT YOUR TRASH CORRECTLY.

DON'T THROW THINGS AWAY. Sell or donate items so they can continue to be helpful. The same goes for shopping: check for second-hand items before buying new ones.

TURN OFF LIGHTS AND WATER when you're not using them.

I Am Nature

Humans are an integral part of nature. We're connected to it in many ways, even if we can't always see it. Without clean air and water, even living in a palace would be impossible. The beauty and balance of nature are at the core of our inner peace and happiness. The further we drift from nature, the less we feel connected to the world and ourselves.

LIVE BY THE PRINCIPLES OF MINDFUL CONSUMPTION. It's not trendy anymore to buy everything just because others have it. This behavior is like a kid collecting rocks to look heavier. What's modern and intelligent now is showing awareness of the new era: not upgrading your phone every year and not buying your tenth pair of jeans or fifth pair of shoes.

CUT BACK ON ANIMAL-BASED PRODUCTS (MEAT, EGGS, MILK). Livestock farming and agriculture are responsible for 24% of annual greenhouse gas emissions. You don't have to give up meat or eggs entirely. Maybe you just decide to eat them only on Fridays or skip your morning omelet. Reducing your consumption of these products is essential to the fight to save the planet.

We tend to see environmental problems as too big to handle, expecting those in power to solve them for us. But in reality, it's up to each of us to bring back the love in our relationship with nature. Your move!

What's next?

Take a moment to think:

- How can you help the planet right now? Make a list of small actions you can take.

- Could your passion be beneficial to the planet? Could it even become socially significant work for you?

- What kind of world do you want to live in 20 years from now? Visualize it.

Take action:

- Get rid of items you don't need or organize a swap with your friends.

- Find a place in your area where you can recycle batteries. Start collecting them separately.

- Reduce the amount of time you spend in the shower. Remember to turn off the tap while brushing your teeth.

Reading material:

- "21 Lessons for the 21st Century" by Yuval Noah Harari

- "Enlightenment Now" by Steven Pinker

- "We Are the Weather: Saving the Planet Begins at Breakfast" by Jonathan Safran Foer

- "The Uninhabitable Earth: Life After Warming" by David Wallace-Wells

- "A Zero Waste Life" by Anita Vandyke

Emma Bryce's TED Talk
on **"What Really Happens to the Plastic You Throw Away?"**

Watch and learn:

Bill Gates's TED Talk
on **"Innovating to Zero!"**

Hans and Ola Rosling's TED Talk
on **"How Not to Be Ignorant About the World"**

Sources

Chapter 1

1. Berne E. **Games People Play: The Psychology of Human Relationships.** — London: Penguin Life, 2016.

2. Bento C. Leal III. **4 Essential Keys to Effective Communication in Love, Life, Work — Anywhere!** — CreateSpace, Independent Publishing Platform, 2017.

3. Marshall B. Rosenberg. **Nonviolent Communication: A Language of Life: Life-Changing Tools for Healthy Relationships.** — Encinitas: PuddleDancer Press, 2015.

4. Sorensen M. **I Hear You: The Surprisingly Simple Skill Behind Extraordinary Relationships.** — Lehi: Autumn Creek Press, 2017.

5. Goleman D. **Emotional Intelligence: Why It Can Matter More Than IQ.** — New York: Random House Publishing Group, 2005.

6. Shapiro D. **Negotiating the Nonnegotiable: How to Resolve Your Most Emotionally Charged Conflicts.** — London: Penguin Books, 2017.

7. Cole T. **Boundary Boss: The Essential Guide to Talk True, Be Seen, and (Finally) Live Free.** — Louisville: Sounds True, 2023.

8. Levin N. **Setting Boundaries Will Set You Free: The Ultimate Guide to Telling the Truth, Creating Connection, and Finding Freedom.** — Carlsbad: Hay House Inc., 2021.

9. Stone D., Heen S. **Thanks for the Feedback: The Science and Art of Receiving Feedback Well.** — London: Penguin Books, 2015.

10. Scott E. **What Is a Toxic Relationship?** // Verywellmind.com.

11. Ducharme J. **How to Tell If You're in a Toxic Relationship — And What to Do About It** // Time.com.

12. Manson M. **6 signs You're in a Toxic Relationship** // Markmanson.net.

Chapter 2

13. Kross E. **Chatter: The Voice in Our Head, Why It Matters, and How to Harness It.** — New York: Crown, 2022.

14. Breuning L. G. **Habits of a Happy Brain: Retrain Your Brain to Boost Your Serotonin, Dopamine, Oxytocin, & Endorphin Levels.** — Avon: Adams Media, 2015.

15. Schwartz R. **No Bad Parts: Healing Trauma and Restoring Wholeness with the Internal Family Systems Model.** — Louisville: Sounds True, 2021.

16. Babich A. **Inner Support.** — Moscow: MIF, 2022 [in Russian].

17. Sand I. **The Emotional Compass.** — Philadelphia: Jessica Kingsley Publishers, 2016.

18. Smith J. **Why Has Nobody Told Me This Before?** — San Francisco: HarperOne, 2022.

19. Mendius R., Hanson R. **Buddha's Brain: The Practical Neuroscience of Happiness, Love, and Wisdom.** — Oakland: New Harbinger Publications, 2009.

20. Singer M. **The Untethered Soul: The Journey Beyond Yourself.** — Oakland: New Harbinger Publications, 2013.

21. Peterson J. **12 Rules for Life: An Antidote to Chaos.** — New York: Random House LCC US, 2018.

22. Schur M. **How to Be Perfect: The Correct Answer to Every Moral Question.** — New York: Simon & Schuster, 2023.

23. Cain S. **Quiet: The Power of Introverts in a World That Can't Stop Talking.** — New York: Crown, 2013.

24. Covey S. **The 7 Habits of Highly Effective Teens: The Ultimate Teenage Success Guide.** — Phoenix: Fireside Publishing, 1998.

25. Harris D. **10% Happier Revised Edition: How I Tamed the Voice in My Head, Reduced Stress Without Losing My Edge, and Found Self-Help That Actually Works — A True Story.** — New York: Dey Street Books, 2019.

26. Paul S. **The Wisdom of Anxiety: How Worry and Intrusive Thoughts Are Gifts to Help You Heal.** — Louisville: Sounds True, 2019.

27. Seligman M. **Learned Optimism: How to Change Your Mind and Your Life.** — New York: Vintage, 2006.

28. Skeen M., Skeen K. **Just As You Are: A Teen's Guide to Self-Acceptance and Lasting Self-Esteem.** — Oakland: Instant Help, 2018.

29. Rae T. **It's OK Not to Be OK: A Guide to Wellbeing.** — London: QED Publishing, 2020.

30. Butovskaya M. **Anthropology of Gender.** — Moscow: Vek-2, 2013 [in Russian].

31. Shainna A. **The Self-Love Workbook: A Life-Changing Guide to Boost Self-Esteem, Recognize Your Worth and Find Genuine Happiness.** — Berkeley: Ulysses Press, 2022.

32. Kaufman G., Espeland P., Raphael L. **Stick Up for Yourself: Every Kid's Guide to Personal Power & Positive Self-Esteem.** — Minneapolis: Free Spirit Publishing, 1999.

33. Bauer B. **You Were Not Born to Suffer.** — London: Watkins Publishing, 2007.

34. Sincero J. **You Are a Badass: How to Stop Doubting Your Greatness and Start Living an Awesome Life.** — Philadelphia: Running Press Adult, 2013.

35. Little B. **Me, Myself, and Us: The Science of Personality and the Art of Well-Being.** — New York: PublicAffairs, 2016.

36. MacCutcheon M. **Self-Esteem Tools for Teens: A Modern Guide to Conquer Your Inner Critic and Realize Your True Self Worth.** — New York: Rockridge Press, 2020.

37. Mate G. **The Myth of Normal: Trauma, Illness, and Healing in a Toxic Culture.** — London: Penguin Audio, 2022.

38. Kay K., Shipman C. **The Confidence Code for Girls: Taking Risks, Messing Up, & Becoming Your Amazingly Imperfect, Totally Powerful Self.** — London: HarperCollins, 2018.

39. **Authenticity** // Psychologytoday.com.

40. **Authenticity. How to Be True to Yourself** // Mindtools.com.

Chapter 3

41. Perry P. **The Book You Wish Your Parents Had Read (and Your Children Will Be Glad That You Did).** — London: Penguin Life, 2020.

42. Newmark D. **How To Raise Emotionally Healthy Children: Meeting The Five Critical Needs of Children… And Parents Too!** — Tarzana: NMI Publisher, 2008.

43. Leviny A., Heller R. **Attached: The New Science of Adult Attachment and How It Can Help You Find — and Keep — Love.** — New York: TarcherPerigee, 2012.

44. Neufeld G., Mate G. **Hold On to Your Kids: Why Parents Need to Matter More Than Peers.** — New York: Ballantine Books, 2006.

45. Petranovskaya L. **When Your Child Is Being Difficult.** — Moscow: AST, 2013 [in Russian].

46. Stixrud W., Johnson N. **The Self-Driven Child: The Science and Sense of Giving Your Kids More Control Over Their Lives.** — London: Penguin Life, 2019.

47. Skynner R., Cleese J. **Families and How to Survive Them.** — London: Vermilion, 1993.

48. Wolynn M. **It Didn't Start with You: How Inherited Family Trauma Shapes Who We Are and How to End the Cycle.** — London: Penguin Audio, 2022.

49. Campbell R. **How to Really Love Your Child.** — Colorado Springs: David C. Cook, 2015.

50. Petranovskaya L. **Generational Trauma** // Pravmir.ru [in Russian].

51. Petranovskaya L. **How to Raise and Not Raise Teenagers** // Pravmir.ru [in Russian].

52. Kamol'dinova G. **My Parents Don't Understand Me** // Pomoschryadom.ru [in Russian].

53. Khlomov K. **Parents and Teens: How to Understand Each Other** // Postnauka.org [in Russian].

54. RTVI. **Everything About Generational Problems** // YouTube.com [in Russian].

55. Henriques M. **Can the Legacy of Trauma be Passed Down the Generations?** // Bbc.com.

56. **Learn About Bowen Theory** // Thebowencenter.org.

57. Kluger J. **The Sibling Bond** // Ted.com.

58. Stephens R. **Building a Strong Family Team: 3 Fundamental Techniques** // Raisingfamilies.org.

Chapter 4

59. Carnegie D. **How to Win Friends & Influence People.** — New York: Pocket Books, 1998.

60. Denworth L. **Friendship: The Evolution, Biology, and Extraordinary Power of Life's Fundamental Bond.** — New York: W. W. Norton & Company, 2021.

61. Brown B. **Daring Greatly: How the Courage to Be Vulnerable Transforms the Way We Live, Love, Parent, and Lead.** — New York: Avery, 2015.

62. Crist J. **The Survival Guide for Making and Being Friends.** — Minneapolis: Free Spirit Publishing, 2014.

63. Faith G. Harper. **Unfuck Your Friendships: Using Science to Make and Maintain the Most Important Relationships of Your Life.** — Cleveland: Microcosm Publishing, 2021.

64. Covey S. **The 6 Most Important Decisions You'll Ever Make: A Guide for Teens.** — New York: Simon & Schuster, 2017.

65. Fitzsimons K. **The Teen's Guide to Social Skills: Practical Advice for Building Empathy, Self-Esteem, and Confidence.** — New York: Rockridge Press, 2021.

66. Ciarrochi J., Hayes L. **Your Life, Your Way: Acceptance and Commitment Therapy Skills to Help Teens Manage Emotions and Build Resilience.** — London: Instant Help, 2020.

67. Erko A. **Friendship with a Catch: How Friends Change Our Lives for the Worse** // Theoryandpractice.ru [in Russian].

68. Samarina M. **Protecting Yourself: 3 Types of Personal Boundaries** // Mel.fm [in Russian].

69. Voiskunsky A. **How Does Online Communication Differ from Offline Communication?** // Postnauka.org [in Russian].

70. Brown B. **The Power of Vulnerability** // Ted.com.

Chapter 5

71. Cain S. **Bittersweet: How Sorrow and Longing Make Us Whole.** — New York: Crown, 2022.

72. Bourbeau L. **Amour — Amour — Amour — La puissance de l'acceptation.** — Paris: ETC, 2021.

73. Johnson S. **Hold Me Tight: Seven Conversations for a Lifetime of Love.** — Boston: Little, Brown Spark, 2008.

74. Aguirre L., O'Sullivan G. **The Girl's Guide to Relationships, Sexuality, and Consent: Tools to Help Teens Stay Safe, Empowered, and Confident.** — Oakland: Instant Help, 2022.

75. Hendrix H., Hunt H. **Getting the Love You Want: A Guide for Couples.** — New York: St. Martin's Griffin, 2019.

76. Chapman G. **The 5 Love Languages. The Secret to Love that Lasts.** — Chicago: Northfield Publishing, 2015.

77. Schnarch D. **Passionate Marriage: Keeping Love and Intimacy Alive in Committed Relationships.** — New York: W.W. Norton & Company, 2019.

78. Milton J. **Lost Yourself in a Relationship? 11 Proven Steps to Find Yourself Again** // Practicalintimacy.com.

79. McHugh S. V. **6 Signs You Have Lost Your Identity** // E-counseling.com.

80. Steber C. **7 Tips for Being Yourself in a New Relationship** // Bustle.com.

Chapter 6

81. Maxwell J. **The 5 Levels of Leadership: Proven Steps to Maximize Your Potential.** — New York City: Center Street, 2013.

82. Fleming K. **Leader's Guide to Emotional Agility: How to Use Soft Skills to Get Hard Results.** — London: FT Publishing International, 2015.

83. Stanley M. **Obedience to Authority: An Experimental View.** — New York: Perennial, 2019.

84. Zhukov D. **Stop! Who's Leading?** — Moscow: Alpina Publisher, 2007 [in Russian].

85. Cialdini R. **Influence: The Psychology of Persuasion.** — New York: Harper Business, 2006.

86. Sapolsky R. **Monkeyluv: And Other Essays on Our Lives as Animals.** — New York City: Scribner, 2005.

87. Sapolsky R. **Behave: The Biology of Humans at Our Best and Worst.** — London: Penguin Books, 2018.

88. Adizes I. **The Ideal Executive: Why You Cannot Be One and What to Do About It, A New Paradigm for Management.** — Carpinteria: Adizes Inst, 2004.

89. Heifetz R., Linsky M. **Leadership on the Line: Staying Alive Through the Dangers of Change.** — Massachusetts: Harvard Business Review Press, 2017.

Chapter 7

90. Kolbert E. **Under a White Sky: The Nature of the Future.** — New York: Crown, 2022.

91. Pinker S. **Enlightenment Now: The Case for Reason, Science, Humanism, and Progress.** — London: Penguin Books, 2019.

92. Foer J. **We Are the Weather: Saving the Planet Begins at Breakfast.** — London: Picador, 2020.

93. Seferian S. M. **Sustainable Minimalism: Embrace Zero Waste, Build Sustainability Habits That Last, and Become a Minimalist Without Sacrificing the Planet.** — London: Mango Media, 2021.

94. Friedman J. **The Next 100 Years: A Forecast for the 21st Century.** — Hamburg: Anchor, 2010.

95. Harari Y. **Sapiens: A Brief History of Humankind.** — New York: Harper Perennial, 2018.

96. Harari Y. **Homo Deus: A Brief History of Tomorrow.** — New York: Harper Perennial, 2018.

97. Harari Y. **21 Lessons for the 21st Century.** — New York: Random House Publishing Group, 2019.

98. Pinker S. **The Better Angels of Our Nature: Why Violence Has Declined.** — London: Penguin Books, 2012.

99. Bill Gates. **Innovating to Zero!** // Ted.com.

100. Jane McGonigal. **Gaming Can Make a Better World** // Ted.com.

An educational visual book for children of middle/high school age and young adults

RELATIONSHIPS. THE VISUAL BOOK FOR TEENS AND TWEENS

Creator of original concept and editor-in-chief *Maria Gorina*
Responsible for publishing *Yulia Antipova*
Translated by *Anna Malyutina*

Printed in Mexico.

For more information contact:
ivigreen.com
hello@ivigreen.com

ISBN 978-1-7378751-6-1